S0-BMW-470

WITHDRAWN

A HISTORY OF THE Z. SMITH REYNOLDS FOUNDATION

ZACHARY SMITH REYNOLDS

November 4, 1911 — July 6, 1932

by BRYAN HAISLIP

A HISTORY OF THE Z. SMITH REYNOLDS FOUNDATION

JOHN F. BLAIR, *Publisher*   *Winston-Salem 1967*

© Copyright 1967 by John Harden Associates
All Rights Reserved
Library of Congress Catalog Card Number: 67–22428

361.7
H 12 h
59035
Sept. 1967

Printed in the United States of America by Kingsport Press, Inc.
Kingsport, Tennessee

*In grateful memory for the years
of leadership, for the thought,
energy, and time each has given
to the works recorded here,
we, the Board of Trustees of the
Z. Smith Reynolds Foundation,
dedicate this history*

TO WILLIAM N. REYNOLDS
MARY REYNOLDS BABCOCK
RICHARD J. REYNOLDS, JR.

CONTENTS

ILLUSTRATIONS

*The majority of the photographs in this book were made by Hugh Morton.
Most of the photographs of the Reynolds family were by Ray W. Goodrich.*

PREFACE

TIME HAS A variable quality. The child feels the year will never pass, while the adult thinks how fast it flies. Thirty years is a brief span for a Foundation created to serve without end. For a man, it is close to half of his Biblically allotted three score and ten.

Time does pass, for men and institutions. As it goes, it takes some of the record. When only memory is the guide, it is difficult or impossible to assess the achievements of either men or corporate bodies. When enterprises of significant impact upon society are involved, and there is no attempt made to gather and preserve the record, history is poorer. Then, indeed, time has been a thief for the generations to come.

It does not seem a long time ago, a hot August day in 1936, when my sisters and I met with the first trustees of the Foundation in Winston-Salem to give reality to our plans to honor the memory of our brother, Z. Smith Reynolds. Present on that occasion were William R. Hubner, Vice President of Safe-Deposit & Trust Company, Baltimore, Md.; William N. Reynolds, our uncle, and Stratton Coyner, my personal lawyer, who was elected secretary of the Foundation.

Still, a review of what the Z. Smith Reynolds Foundation has been able to achieve since that day makes it seem as though it has been a very long time. A pioneer program to control venereal disease, the moving of Wake Forest College westward more than 100 miles, Smith Reynolds Airport, Tanglewood Park, programs in scholarship and education—and many other projects in process or completed—have been a part of the eventful 30 years.

The trustees of the Foundation have no personal motives in the preparation and publication of this history. We have received our satisfaction. Whatever fond hopes we entertained, as we formally created the memorial to Smith, have been more than exceeded in the Foundation's achievements.

Rather, the obligation we feel is to the future. The Foundation has been engaged in undertakings which have made, and will continue to make, lasting changes in the face and character of North Carolina. It is only proper that the record should be preserved, so that all North Carolinians, present and yet to come, might know how these things came into being.

Finally, it is in keeping with the Foundation's purpose as a memorial that this history be set down. Smith Reynolds died before his 21st birthday—a brief life. Through this Foundation, and its achievements recorded here, his memory and name will remain forever alive.

RICHARD J. REYNOLDS, JR., *President*   (April 4, 1906 – December 14, 1964)

My brother, Richard J. Reynolds, Jr., was keenly interested in the preparation of the history of the Z. Smith Reynolds Foundation. Indeed, the Foundation itself from the time of its creation was one of the principal interests of his life.

Only a few weeks before his death, Dick and I spent hours together at his home in Emmetten, Switzerland, going over a first draft of a portion of the history. The Preface immediately above was one of the last tasks to which he gave attention. He gave it great care, and I have felt it should remain as he finally left it.

Dick's vision for the Foundation was centered on people. He wanted to see it help them, in tangible ways which they could understand. Then, he hoped it might lead them to help others. He felt a history would show how this had been accomplished, and so remind us that it should continue to be our concern.

NANCY REYNOLDS VERNEY, *President, January 2, 1967*

ACKNOWLEDGMENTS

THE Z. SMITH REYNOLDS Foundation, since it came into being thirty years ago, has touched many people and many institutions in the state of North Carolina. Public officials, educators, physicians, ministers, lawyers, businessmen, and plain citizens have been drawn into its work and have shared in its achievements. To them I wish to express my grateful appreciation. Without their help this history could not have been written.

There are a few whose special assistance merits particular acknowledgment. They have granted personal interviews, opened private files of correspondence and other material, and aided the preparation of the history in a variety of ways.

Hon. Capus Waynick of Fieldstone Farm, High Point, gave important help in developing the chapter on the venereal disease control project. Valuable assistance came also from Dr. J. W. R. Norton, State Health Director for North Carolina, and James W. Hicks, chief of the venereal disease control section of the state health department.

President Harold W. Tribble of Wake Forest College was a source of courteous and unfailing assistance for the chapter dealing with the college. Others of the college who contributed included Dr. Coy C. Carpenter, vice-president for medical affairs; Dr. Henry S. Stroupe, director of graduate studies; Eugene I. Olive, director emeritus of alumni activities; Worth H. Copeland, secretary and treasurer of the trustees; and Russell H. Brantley, Jr., director of communications.

Among those not directly connected with the college administration who gave assistance, special mention should be made of

Judge Johnson J. Hayes, of Wilkesboro, and Irving E. Carlyle, of Winston-Salem.

Charles E. Norfleet, of Winston-Salem, shared his intimate knowledge of the development of the Z. Smith Reynolds Airport. Arthur Graham, airport manager, also contributed vital facts and statistics.

Gardner Gidley, former superintendent of Tanglewood Park, opened his extensive file of material on the park for use in preparing that part of the history.

President D. Grier Martin and his staff at Davidson College gave valuable assistance and guidance concerning the Foundation's activities there, while Chancellor John T. Caldwell and R. W. Shoffner, director of foundations and development, performed the same kind of service for North Carolina State University, Raleigh, a unit of the Consolidated University of North Carolina.

The Winston-Salem Journal and Sentinel and the Winston-Salem Public Library made available their files on the Foundation and its programs.

Finally, the trustees of the Foundation themselves have contributed to the history, both in data and in guidance. Nancy Reynolds Verney and William R. Lybrook have given step-by-step supervision of the project. Others among the trustees deserving particular mention include Richard J. Reynolds, Jr., who until his death followed with keen interest the preparation of the history; Charles H. Babcock, whose insight into the Foundation's role and function was especially valuable; and L. D. Long, whose close association with W. N. Reynolds gave particular importance to his contributions.

Stratton Coyner, of Winston-Salem, first secretary to the Foundation trustees and himself a trustee for many years, provided a wealth of background detail. Ledyard S. Staples, present secretary, made available minutes and records of the Foundation which gave much of the framework for the history.

John Harden and other staff members of John Harden Associates have also contributed to the preparation of the history.

Assembling the record of the Z. Smith Reynolds Foundation has been an exciting and satisfying assignment. I believe this volume serves a valuable purpose in preserving for the years ahead important scenes from the social history of North Carolina. All who have had a part in it have rendered a distinct service to their state, and the realization that they have done so is their real reward.

BRYAN HAISLIP

A HISTORY OF THE Z. SMITH REYNOLDS FOUNDATION

CORNERSTONES I
How It Began

BOLDNESS AND IMAGINATION were characteristics of Zachary Smith Reynolds, younger son of the founder of the R. J. Reynolds Tobacco Company. His enthusiasm for flying was typical. He was an accomplished pilot while still in his teens, at a time when aviation was barely out of the pioneer stage.

These same qualities have distinguished the Z. Smith Reynolds Foundation, created by his brother and two sisters after his tragic and early death.

In dramatic and often daring ways, the Foundation has been active for three decades now in promoting a fuller, more useful life for North Carolinians. Because no previous effort has been made to draw together the record, few citizens of the state are even aware of the range and scope of the Foundation's achievements. This brief history is designed to tell the story of the Foundation's role in advancing health, education, and the general public good in North Carolina.

"The object for which this corporation is formed is the accomplishment of charitable works in the State of North Carolina."

These formal words are in the charter filed August 21, 1936, with North Carolina Secretary of State Stacey Wade in Raleigh. The trustees quickly demonstrated their intention to give dynamic interpretation to the Foundation's purpose and to involve it significantly in the life of the state.

The first project selected was a campaign to wipe out venereal disease in North Carolina. To achieve the objective, the Foundation pledged its entire income to the State Board of Health. This frontal attack on a problem that had remained largely shadowed and unmentionable until that time brought headlines in newspapers of North Carolina and beyond. The action was hailed as a milestone in private support of public health work.

"We feel the time has come when something should be done," said Richard J. Reynolds, Jr., Foundation president, in a news account of the initial grant, "and we believe that if a proper program is carried out over a number of years results will be obtained. . . . We hope that we will be able to aid in the campaign to eradicate syphilis."

For nearly a decade the venereal disease program was the Foundation's major concern. Then its attention turned to the field of education and an ambitious and daring undertaking. This was the proposal to move Wake Forest College to Winston-Salem. Many persons, within and without the ranks of Baptists, said that an institution more than a hundred years old could not survive a transfer to a site more than a hundred miles distant. Wake Forest did, and now flourishes in its adopted community.

These two projects—both of which made a tremendous impact upon North Carolina—serve to illustrate the imagination which has guided the trustees of the Z. Smith Reynolds Foundation. They are also representative of the Foundation's mainstreams of interest, public health and public education.

Charles H. Babcock, himself a trustee of long standing, recalls that his wife, Mary Reynolds Babcock, held firmly to the philosophy that health and education were the proper spheres for good works, "feeling that with good health and good education everyone could become self-supporting."

The principle the founders sought to lay down in choosing

North Carolina as their area of activity has been aptly stated by Nancy Reynolds Verney. "This wealth was created in North Carolina," Mrs. Verney said. "It was the feeling of all those concerned, I think, that its benefits should go back to North Carolina and to North Carolinians, who helped create it."

Time and wise investments have richly increased the resources from which the Foundation draws its income. W. N. Reynolds, uncle of the founders and their close adviser, created by a bequest a trust whose income goes to the Foundation.

While health and education have been guiding goals for the Foundation, the trustees have followed insight rather than orthodoxy in making grants. For example, they have aided the Old Salem restoration, which might be classified as education in view of the thousands of school children it has enthralled with visual history. Tanglewood Park, another beneficiary, could be considered a public health project on the ground that wholesome recreation is a direct contribution to a community's good health.

Community betterment has been a constant concern for the Foundation, both in state-wide and in local terms. By charter its activities are limited to North Carolina. Emphasis is upon those programs that are state-wide in scope. Yet, its location in Winston-Salem and the Reynolds family's identification with the area give a particular sensitivity to local needs and civic enterprises.

The first important project in this direction was the development of an airport to serve Winston-Salem and Forsyth County. The result was the Z. Smith Reynolds Airport, an appropriate memorial to Smith Reynolds' keen interest in aviation. Foundation trustees and local officials felt assured that the airport would secure main-line air service for the community. That it did not (and it did until recently) was due to circumstances beyond their foresight and control.

There have been many other instances of the Foundation's sense of involvement with the Winston-Salem area. A recent one is its support of the North Carolina School of the Arts. Here, it is well to note, local and state-wide service is joined; while the school is situated in Winston-Salem, its students come from all over the state — indeed, from the whole Southern region.

In similar manner, the scholarship programs sponsored by the Foundation are spreading its influence in many directions: doctors trained at the Bowman Gray School of Medicine (the Reynolds scholarships there are among the most generous available in the country), young women prepared for teaching and other fields at the University of North Carolina at Greensboro, Negro youth given opportunities for study at Bennett and Livingstone Colleges.

No better example of the Foundation's freshness of vision, and its abiding commitment to service within its state, could be given than its partnership in the creation of the North Carolina Fund as an attempt to "break the cycle of poverty."

It is not the purpose here to list all the activities in which the Foundation has played a part. This is done elsewhere in this volume. The listing shows how the Foundation has reached into all parts of the state through many grants, some of them small, to hospitals, schools, colleges, and other institutions.

A striking aspect of the Z. Smith Reynolds Foundation has been its concentration upon purpose rather than procedure. The trustees have kept foremost the Foundation's aim of service to North Carolina, developing only the essential minimum of administrative machinery. This has left both their attention, and the funds they find available, free for the furtherance of projects.

Thus, while $30,919,398 had been spent by the Foundation through 1966 for education, health, and other causes, administrative expenses were only approximately $142,300.20, or less than $\frac{1}{2}$ of 1 per cent. Since its creation, the Foundation's annual income has grown from less than $200,000 to more than $2,000,000.

CORNERSTONES
How It Began

In a basic sense, the Foundation is a family undertaking and a family responsibility. This has permitted an informality of operation and has given a strong continuity in membership of trustees. Relatives of Z. Smith Reynolds who have served have included the brother and two sisters who set up the Foundation, an uncle, a nephew, a cousin, and—in recent years—a daughter. Other trustees have been related by marriage, close personal friends, or business associates.

These have been people who knew Smith Reynolds, directly or through family and business connections. Their deep and personal

Skyline of Winston-Salem, home of the Z. Smith Reynolds Foundation

interest in his memorial has been reflected in the dedication they give to their responsibilities as trustees.

The first recorded document in the Foundation's history is a letter dated April 14, 1933, to W. N. Reynolds.

DEAR UNCLE WILL:

Having heretofore agreed between ourselves upon a common desire to establish, out of the trust funds created by the wills of our father and mother for the benefit of our brother, Smith Reynolds, to which we may now be entitled and of which we may hereafter obtain possession, a trust for charitable, benevolent and eleemosynary purposes in the state of North Carolina, we write to confirm that agreement.

It is our common intention, as agreed between us, to create such a trust whenever our dominion over and title to such estates, in whole or in part, is conceded or judicially declared to be such as to legally enable and entitle us to do it.

Save for the purpose named, we do not expect to claim or receive any part of such estates, other than such sum as is necessary to reimburse us for expenses incurred.

The sole reason for our participation in the litigation now pending over this property, distasteful as it will doubtless be, is to do what we can to make effective this plan, thus honoring and perpetuating the memory of our brother, Smith.

We understand Mrs. Smith Reynolds and the mother and grandparents of Anne Cannon Reynolds, 2nd, are in accord with this plan.

Affectionately,

(signed)   RICHARD J. REYNOLDS
(signed)   MARY REYNOLDS BABCOCK
(signed)   NANCY REYNOLDS BAGLEY

The intention to create the Foundation was approved by the North Carolina Supreme Court, in a decision which ended litigation over the Smith Reynolds estate. Associate Justice Heroit Clarkson, writing the opinion handed down at the 1935 fall term, said the compromise settlement—in which the Foundation proposal was a key item—was "fair, just and equitable." He continued: "In this jurisdiction the Courts, for perhaps a hundred years, have upheld family settlements, and the general policy of the Courts has been to encourage compromise of litigation."

With the way legally cleared, the brother and sisters proceeded with organization of the Foundation. Papers of incorporation were filed August 21, 1936, with the North Carolina Secretary of State, Stacey W. Wade, in Raleigh. On the same day in Winston-Salem the three original incorporators and trustees convened their initial meeting. A first act was the election of two additional trustees. One of these was W. N. Reynolds, uncle of the incorporators. The other was W. R. Hubner of the Safe Deposit and Trust Company, Baltimore, Maryland, trustee for the Zachary Smith Reynolds Trust.

Officers chosen at this first meeting were Richard J. Reynolds, Jr., president, W. N. Reynolds, vice-president, and Stratton Coyner, secretary.

Securities valued as of May 12, 1936, at $7,210,887.51 were placed in the Zachary Smith Reynolds Trust, with the income to be paid to the Foundation. Twenty per cent of the income was to be retained and added to the trust, until a total of $50,000,000 should be reached.

Accordingly, the trustees were advised at their meeting on December 2, 1937, that the first income was payable to the Foundation, in the amount of $162,241.39. A resolution was adopted selecting for the first project a program for the control of venereal disease in North Carolina, and a grant of $100,000 to the state health department was approved. With this action, the Foundation became a functioning organization.

Richard J. Reynolds, Jr., first president of the Foundation, served until June, 1942, when he reported to the trustees that he had volunteered for duty with the U.S. Navy. W. N. Reynolds,

The Richard J. Reynolds family. Standing, Mrs. R. J. Reynolds; left to right, Mary, R. J. Reynolds, Nancy, Dick, and Smith

William N. Reynolds, better known as Mr. Will (March 22, 1863—September 10, 1951)

Richard J. Reynolds, Jr. (April 4, 1906—December 14, 1964)

Mary Reynolds Babcock (August 8, 1908—July 17, 1953)

Nancy Reynolds Verney

who had been a guiding influence in setting up the Foundation and remained active in its affairs, was elected president. He held the office until his death on September 10, 1951, at the age of eighty-eight. During this time, the Foundation developed and brought close to reality its second major project — the removal of Wake Forest College to Winston-Salem.

Richard J. Reynolds, Jr., returned from World War II service, again was elected president. Limitations of health made it necessary for him to give up the office, and on October 19, 1964, the trustees elected Nancy Reynolds Verney as president.

The contributions of its second president were recognized by the Foundation in a resolution adopted by the trustees on May 9, 1952. It read:

Mr. W. N. Reynolds, a Trustee and President of this Foundation, passed away on September 10, 1951 in the 88th year of his life.

Mr. Will, as he was affectionately known by his friends and associates, was intensely interested in this Foundation and gave unstintedly of his time and energy to its work. His always wise counsel and advice, as well as his presence, will be sorely missed by the Trustees and others connected with this Foundation.

Mr. Will was widely known, loved and revered throughout his long life for his outstanding qualities of leadership, his thoughtfulness and generosity to his fellow man regardless of race or creed. His many charitable acts, his great interest, guidance and help in civic affairs will long be remembered.

A man of truly great stature in every respect has passed on to his reward.

At this same meeting the trustees were told that W. N. Reynolds left assurance of his continued support for the Z. Smith Reynolds Foundation in his will, which created a charitable trust with principal of approximately $14,000,000 and income payable to the Foundation. At present, the trust is valued at $41,500,000.

Death removed one of the three founders of the Foundation,

THE Z. SMITH REYNOLDS FOUNDATION   15

Mary Reynolds Babcock, on July 17, 1953. The following December, the trustees by resolution designated grants made at that meeting in her memory "in recognition of her kindness and thoughtfulness towards others which characterized her life and works."

Mary Reynolds Babcock gave her time and talents to the Z. Smith Reynolds Foundation, and also contributed to its financial growth. Her gifts added $1,324,000 to the Zachary Smith Reynolds Trust. In addition, her gifts were responsible for income to the Foundation totaling $1,981,560.

With her husband, Charles H. Babcock, she carried on an active role in the Foundation's affairs. They made available a portion of their estate, Reynolda, as the new campus for Wake Forest College in its relocation. They also served as hosts at Reynolda for President Harry S. Truman when he came to Winston-Salem to participate in the groundbreaking for the new campus.

The original incorporators are trustees for life. By-laws provide for a membership of no less than three nor more than fifteen. At present, there are ten trustees. It is a self-elective group, with specified terms.

Charles H. Babcock and L. D. Long, an associate of W. N. Reynolds, have served as trustees since April 24, 1946. Thomas B. Butler of the Safe Deposit and Trust Company, Baltimore, was elected April 15, 1948, upon the resignation of W. R. Hubner. William R. Lybrook and Stratton Coyner were elected December 4, 1953. William R. Lybrook is vice-president and secretary of the R. J. Reynolds Tobacco Company. Stratton Coyner, for many years an associate of Richard J. Reynolds and Foundation secretary in its early years, has since resigned as a Foundation trustee. Henry Walker Bagley served as a trustee for the period 1946–1953.

Anne Reynolds Forsyth, the daughter of Z. Smith Reynolds, has been a trustee since May 31, 1958. Smith Walker Bagley, son of

Nancy Reynolds Verney, was elected a trustee on December 2, 1959.

Three trustees were elected on October 21, 1966. They are Joseph W. Lineberger, Katharine Babcock Mountcastle, and Zachary Taylor Smith.

The trustees generally meet in spring and fall, often in Winston-Salem. They review projects, consider requests for Foundation participation in new programs, and take action to make funds available for selected purposes. Ledyard S. Staples, secretary and treasurer, maintains records of the proceedings and keeps the trustees informed on requests received and other matters.

The Foundation staff consists of the part-time services of Mr. Staples, who also served as secretary to Richard J. Reynolds, Jr., and such secretarial assistance as is needed. Much of the work on behalf of the Foundation has been and is still handled by the unpaid trustees.

In this way, the Foundation has been able to concentrate its resources upon its objectives without the feeling of lost motion or wasted energy. The trustees feel confident that this has been a factor in its accomplishments.

LIFTING THE SHADOW II

A DRAMATIC AND DIRECT ATTACK upon the number one health problem of the time was the initial project of the Z. Smith Reynolds Foundation. The target was venereal disease, a scourge feared and difficult to combat because it had been kept out of public sight and mentioned only in whispers. Nor was the Foundation's enlistment a token one; its total income was pledged to the North Carolina State Board of Health for the war on syphilis and gonorrhea.

The trustees approved the first grant of $100,000 to the State Board of Health on December 2, 1937. The program continued for nearly a decade, with the final grant on April 24, 1946, bringing the total supplied by the Foundation to $1,535,000.

This period embraced both World War II, with the social upheaval and military movements of men which intensified the hazards of venereal disease, and the discovery of drugs and treatment procedures which greatly simplified its cure. At the close of the period, venereal disease was no longer the dreaded destroyer it had been. It was not eliminated, but it was under more effective public health controls. Most important, it was in the open, as an acknowledged health menace which could be dealt with frankly.

The Foundation's involvement in venereal disease control had its origin in the impact of a book of the mid-1930's by Dr. Thomas Parran, titled *The Shadow on the Land.* Dr. Parran, surgeon general of the U.S. Public Health Service, warned of the spread of syphilis throughout the nation and its toll on national health. He pleaded for an end to public blindness and indifference to the threat.

Mary Reynolds Babcock read a magazine article dealing with Dr. Parran's campaign and became convinced of the need for action. Charles H. Babcock recalls that his wife took a keen interest in the American Social Hygiene Association, which was beginning to bring into the open the problem of venereal diseases.

"She personally financed with a $50,000 grant to the American Social Hygiene Association the starting of what became National Social Hygiene Day throughout the country," he said. "This was to encourage local effort toward doing something about the venereal disease situation."

Other members of the family caught her enthusiasm. When the Foundation was ready to select its first undertaking, venereal disease control seemed the logical choice.

Dr. Carl V. Reynolds, state health officer and no relation to the family, hailed the step as a call to "war on 'the Great Exterminator,' a disease that has shown humanity no mercy." Newspaper accounts described it as the largest gift for public health purposes ever made in the South. Richard J. Reynolds, Jr., president of the Foundation trustees, said it was hoped the campaign would focus national attention on the North Carolina venereal disease control program as a model for the rest of the country.

Dr. Reynolds outlined the scope of North Carolina's venereal disease problem in a proposed control program submitted to the Reynolds Foundation. He estimated that 10 per cent of the state's population (300,000 or more persons) had syphilis, and that gonorrhea was even more general. His estimate was later borne out by medical examination of North Carolina men during the World War II draft.

Complicating the problem, nationally as well as in North Carolina, was the fact that in the 1930's mention of venereal disease was socially taboo. As Buncombe County health officer in 1915, Dr. Carl V. Reynolds had created a stir by his insistence that venereal disease cases be reported as such. Most people preferred that venereal disease not be mentioned, and few doctors reported cases under their care.

Health officials realized that only limited effectiveness could come from a state-wide program. They chose sixteen counties where the need was known, programs could be made adequate, and community and health department cooperation was assured. These were Anson, Buncombe, Cabarrus, Cumberland, Durham, Edgecombe-Greene (district health department), Forsyth, Gaston, Guilford, Mecklenburg, Orange, Robeson, Rowan, Wake, and Wayne counties, plus the city of Rocky Mount. These health departments provided services for approximately one-third of the state's population.

To become eligible for the Reynolds Foundation program, each governmental unit had to sign a twelve-page agreement pledging the cooperation of health officials, the county medical society, county commissioners, the mayor or city manager of each city in the county. It also covered cooperation of welfare agencies, sheriff, and police departments.

Under the agreement, local authorities pledged to do the following things:

Select qualified local private physicians to man their clinic or clinics.

Furnish adequate space for the clinics.

Match Foundation funds dollar for dollar.

Cooperate with the State Board of Health in making a survey to determine the percentage of persons infected in the area, classify the stage of the disease in infected persons, and determine adequacy of treatment.

Furnish the State Board of Health any records or reports required.

There were other provisions, but these serve to show the thoroughness of the state health department's approach.

An excerpt from Dr. Carl V. Reynolds' 1946 report to the Foundation describes the situation in 1937 and underscores the need for such thoroughness:

The control program up to the time of the Foundation gift had accomplished very little more than to bring into partial view the mass of infections that was weakening the state. Treatment with the methods then in use was sporadic, and inadequate to restore the health of any considerable portion of the persons found suffering from the disease. There was no organized case-finding, scant means for holding patients under treatment long enough for clinical care, and practically no provisions for follow-up or contact investigation. . . .

The Z. Smith Reynolds Foundation pointed the way for an effective program for the control of syphilis through cooperation between public health agencies, private medicine, and the community. This pioneer program demonstrated that such a team approach can lead to the control of syphilis. When awareness of the problem is increased and when people learn what can be done about it, community support is increased—which is necessary to the program.

By insisting on matching local funds and other community involvement, the Foundation created both the awareness and the local support necessary to a successful program.

The expressed hope of Richard J. Reynolds, Jr., for nationwide interest to be created by the Foundation was quickly realized. Dr. Reynolds described it in his 1946 report:

The very next year (1938) a North Carolinian, inspired and strengthened by what the Foundation had done in his own state, gave his name and strong support to a federal statute which made a large appropriation for the venereal disease control program. The Bulwinkle-LaFollette bill was passed, making the first important financial provision for federal cooperation with the states in the war on these diseases. . . .

He referred to the Tar Heel co-author of the bill, Congressman A. L. Bulwinkle of Gastonia.

With the passage of the National Venereal Disease Control Act of 1938, on May 24, 1938, the modern venereal disease control program in the United States began. When other states began their programs, they naturally turned to North Carolina for guidance.

In this state, the effect of the Reynolds program was dramatic. *Reported* cases annually ranged from 2,000 in 1919 to 6,000 in 1936. With the start of the Foundation program, reported cases jumped to more than 12,000 in 1937, rose to nearly 21,000 the following year, and reached a peak of 30,000 in 1939.

The first accomplishment of the Foundation program was to bring under treatment a large number of cases contracted before 1938, Dr. Reynolds reported. Up to 1943 the main effect of the program was largely one of treating the great backlog of cases contracted four years or more before the cases were discovered.

World War II brought tremendous population shifts. It created an atmosphere of excitement, emotional stress, and uncertainty that brought on moral laxity and a resulting increase in venereal disease. Further, the armed forces removed from civilian life many trained and experienced personnel in the fields of health and medicine.

Two major benefits came out of the war: the development of Rapid Treatment Centers in 1943 (North Carolina had two of fifty-two in the nation, in Charlotte and Durham), and the discovery of new and more effective drugs that reduced the time for cure from as much as several years to a matter of days (even to a single injection).

In 1946 Reynolds Foundation funds went to sixteen counties with nineteen health jurisdictions. Their total population was 1,232,180, or 35.7 per cent of the state's population that was served by the state's venereal disease program. However, under the stimulus of Reynolds funds, these counties produced 59.9 per cent of the sources of infection traced, 51.1 per cent of the sources examined, and 49.5 per cent of those referred to the Rapid Treatment Centers.

There was a solid reason for such a record. In one year, a study of the personnel employed in the local venereal disease program in the state showed that 170 out of 375 were paid by Foundation funds. These included 54 physicians (6 of them full-time), 61 nurses, and a total of 65 bacteriologists, clerks, and follow-up workers.

State and federal health authorities realized that treatment of known cases, alone, would not bring venereal disease under control. Educational materials were needed to enlist the public's help. In 1942 the Reynolds Foundation joined the U.S.P.H.S. in financing the Venereal Disease Education Institute, operated under the State Board of Health. The Institute's able director, Capus Waynick, was appointed by Dr. Carl V. Reynolds on June 25, 1942.

Waynick, then editor of the *High Point Enterprise,* has reported that it took the personal persuasion of Richard J. Reynolds, Jr., to get him into the job. "Dick Reynolds urged me that there was a war-connected responsibility in the matter that I ought to recognize," Waynick said. "His insistence and earnestness about it and my increasing realization of the nature of the problem caused me to change my mind and I agreed to do the job. . . ."

The Institute had the following assignments:

1. To develop materials for public education in venereal diseases, to aid in control.
2. To demonstrate use of the materials.
3. To evaluate the impact of the materials.

It was largely an uncharted area which Waynick invaded. He recalls that his appeals to public health officials for advice brought the response: "If we could answer those questions we wouldn't need you."

He queried many universities in search of a formula to use in evaluation of health education materials. Uniformly, he was told: "We have none, and if you develop some please let us know." He plunged ahead on his own.

I set up a small group of writers and artists—commercial artists— and began to experiment with so-called educational materials the purpose of which was largely to get the diseases in the open. Throughout all of this work I had the full encouragement of the Reynolds family and the Foundation.

We produced many booklets and posters and as far as I know, for the first time the comic book was utilized as a way of getting the attention of people who needed to be informed. I remember very pleasantly the flood of letters that came to me from doctors throughout the U.S.A., some of them expressing wonder that the comic book hadn't been utilized in this manner before.

The Institute went beyond the U.S. Public Health Service assignment and furnished great masses of its materials to other states, to the U.S. Army, and even to the Canadian Army. Col. Oveta Culp Hobby, commander of the Women's Army Corps (WACS), adopted a booklet titled "What Every Woman Ought to Know" for use among her feminine soldiers and directed the

Institute to produce a large edition under a change of name. Canada bought the same book for distribution to women in the Canadian Army.

The Institute produced booklets, at times in quantities of five or six million each, for use throughout the world. A series of posters, in both English and Spanish, was produced and sent monthly to all U.S. Army installations. Production of the posters ran in quantities of 50,000 each.

Waynick left his post in 1948 to manage the successful campaign for governor of W. Kerr Scott. Later, he served as U.S. Ambassador to Nicaragua and Colombia.

Primary objectives of venereal disease education were threefold: to induce the infected to visit a clinic or private physician for diagnosis and treatment (if needed), to persuade the infected to cooperate in finding other cases by talking frankly, and to hold the patient under treatment until released by a physician.

After four months of training personnel, the Institute started its creative effort. By June 16, 1943, it had produced three booklets; a short play for Negro colleges and schools; a series of radio scripts, speeches and newspaper releases; a questionnaire to evaluate educational materials; twenty posters; and was working on a set of slides. The Institute had spent several weeks demonstrating intensive use of educational material in Cabarrus County. Businessmen cooperated by displaying posters, and the largest department store in Concord volunteered its main street window for a display.

Institute lecturers were welcome in both white and Negro high schools. The State Parent-Teacher Association invited the Institute to have an exhibit and to conduct an open forum at its June 30 annual meeting.

All of this is in dramatic contrast to the days seven years earlier when Dr. Reynolds was trying to get people just to admit the existence of venereal diseases!

THE Z. SMITH REYNOLDS FOUNDATION 25

James W. Hicks, chief of the Venereal Disease Control Section of the State Board of Health, emphasized the Institute's effectiveness with this comment in October, 1964: "Scarcely a day goes by that we do not get a letter addressed to the Venereal Disease Education Institute, although it went out of existence in 1947."

STAIRWAYS OF AIR   III

ON THE AFTERNOON OF AUGUST 26, 1931, a nineteen-year-old pilot took off in an 80-horse-power Savoia-Marchetti amphibian "on what I hope will be a flight that will take me over many foreign countries and to many interesting places."

With these confident words, written in his log, Zachary Smith Reynolds set off on a 17,000-mile, London-to-China air adventure. His remarkable courage and fortitude may be best appreciated by recalling aviation's adolescent state between the World Wars, and the isolated areas of the world over which the flight lay.

He completed the trip, despite difficulties and discouragement. Impressions and incidents of the flight, set down in the log, have been preserved by his sister, Nancy Reynolds Verney, in a privately printed volume.

Aviation was so new when Smith Reynolds began to fly that the government had not yet set up any system to license pilots. Anyone who wanted to fly did so, without regard to age or qualifications. Many pilots felt it was a drawback not to have a license. In case of accident, there was no way to show whether the pilot involved was capable or qualified.

An approach was made to Orville Wright, one of the Dayton, Ohio, brothers and bicycle mechanics who successfully tested their flying machine on the North Carolina coast in man's first flight in heavier-than-air equipment. Under the auspices of the Federale Aeronautique Internationale, he agreed to test pilots who requested it and to issue certificates to those he deemed qualified. Smith Reynolds received one of these licenses while only sixteen years of age. Approximately one year later, when the federal government began to license pilots, he had so much experience that he bypassed a private license and was immediately issued a transport license, which authorized him to fly commercially. He also held a mechanic's license.

His early and intense interest in aviation is perpetuated in the Smith Reynolds Airport at Winston-Salem. In a sense, the airport project involved more personal sentiment than any other Foundation undertaking. It was the first to memorialize his name. Certainly, too, it was a place where he would have felt at home, in sight of the landing and departing planes and sharing the comradely talk of pilots and mechanics.

In the late '30's, communities throughout the country began to awaken to the dawning air age and to plan and develop airports to serve the increasing number of planes the future would bring. Winston-Salem was no exception. Its airport had been started in 1926 with a gift of land from R. E. Lasater and of equipment from A. Clinton Miller. The need for expanded facilities and for airline service continued to engage the attention of civic leaders.

Charles E. Norfleet, a Wachovia Bank and Trust Company official and former president of the Chamber of Commerce, agreed to spearhead community efforts in this direction as chairman of the Chamber's aviation committee. After receiving encouragement from Eastern Air Lines that they would come into Winston-Salem if facilities were adequate, he approached Richard J. Reynolds, Jr. The reaction was favorable. Dick Reynolds took an immediate interest and agreed to bring the matter before the Foundation.

Howard L. Cheney, architect for the National Airport at

Washington, was acknowledged the leading authority in the field of airport design. Reynolds contacted him, and Cheney sent Ben Smith, a member of his staff, to look over the Winston-Salem scene.

"I will never forget it," Norfleet recalled. "Dick, Ben, and I went out to the airport. For some reason, carpenters were working there. After we showed Ben Smith around, he picked up a plank and with a little pencil began to sketch a building on it. Well, Dick liked it very much, and I liked it very much. The next thing I knew, we were looking for a saw. Ben Smith sawed off the plank

Z. Smith Reynolds Airport, Winston-Salem

THE Z. SMITH REYNOLDS FOUNDATION 29

and stuck it in his briefcase, and took it back to Washington with him."

The Foundation trustees in June, 1940, agreed to make available to Forsyth County $150,000 for airport improvements, including the erection of an administration building, the installation of a lighting system, the construction and extension of runways. Prior to Foundation action, Richard J. Reynolds, Jr., had advanced funds to begin the airport project, and he personally gave the land for the extension of the runways.

The *Winston-Salem Journal* reported the Foundation's initial grant in a news article which said the improvements would make possible air-line service for the city. "The gift assures Winston-Salem of early completion of one of the finest airports in the Southeast," the story declared. Norfleet was quoted in the article, expressing appreciation for the Foundation's aid as a step "that undoubtedly will be of untold value to the community both in the immediate future and in the years to come."

Federal W.P.A. funds, through the North Carolina program under C. C. McGinnis of Raleigh, were used in the airport work on a matching basis of approximately two-to-one. Richard J. Reynolds, Jr., reported to the Foundation trustees, meeting in October, 1940, that the improvement project, estimated to cost a total of about $635,000, could be carried out with a grant of around $200,000, exclusive of land. However, the cost of the administration building ran beyond first estimates. At its meeting in June, 1941, the Foundation supplemented its earlier $150,000 participation with an additional $80,000.

The start of World War II, with Pearl Harbor, intervened. Material shortages and other difficulties plagued the project, and it was necessary for the Foundation in June, 1942, to provide another $114,700 for the airport. Another $50,000 supplement was made the following year.

The decision to name it the Smith Reynolds Airport was announced by the Winston-Salem Airport Commission in April, 1942, as it neared completion.

"It seems entirely fitting and proper," said Norfleet, "that the airport should bear the name of Smith Reynolds, in recognition of his early and eager interest in aviation, his accomplishments in this field, and the part which the Foundation bearing his name and created from a portion of his estate has had in building the terminal." Formal dedication of the airport was held June 13, 1942, shortly before Richard J. Reynolds, Jr., then Winston-Salem mayor as well as president of the Foundation trustees, reported for duty with the U.S. Navy.

In a news account of the naming of the airport, the *Winston-Salem Journal* noted that the terminal building was "regarded by many authorities as second only to that in the nation's capital in modern construction, beauty, and efficiency." The article continued: "Airline officials and others familiar with most or all airport terminal buildings in the country have described the one here as outstanding in every way. Bearing in mind the comparative sizes of the two cities, the Winston-Salem building is ranked next to the new Washington terminal."

The war brought a tempo of increased activity to the Smith Reynolds Airport. The Office of Flying Safety moved into the Nissen Building, to give Winston-Salem an added sense of the impending conflict. Heavy demands on the airport by the U.S. Army Air Corps, and other military and defense traffic, brought with it the opportunity for expansion and improvements through federal funds.

Norfleet, as secretary of the Forsyth County Airport Commission, brought these opportunities to the attention of the Foundation. He submitted to the trustees an outline which proposed the purchase of $370,000 worth of land in order to provide for the future development of the airport. Because of the field's use by the Flight Control Command, Norfleet said, if the land were available the federal government would in all probability build and extend the runway system.

The trustees gave sympathetic attention to the development program and agreed to make available to Forsyth County a total of $250,000 over a five-year period. This made possible the purchase of land for the extension of runways and other improvements.

Thus, over a period of about three years, the Foundation provided $644,700 and the stimulus to give Winston-Salem and its area an airport adequate for its dynamic economy.

Eventually, the Smith Reynolds Airport lost its status as a trunk-line airport. After lengthy hearings, the airport at Friendship was designated as the area airport to serve Winston-Salem, Greensboro, and High Point with trunk-line service. Piedmont was directed to continue its service to Smith Reynolds Airport.

Even so, the airport investment continues to pay important dividends for the Winston-Salem area, according to Airport Manager Arthur R. Graham. Statistics from the Federal Aviation Authority, he said, show that Smith Reynolds is the busiest airport in North Carolina in total number of landings and take-offs and ranks 103d among the 278 airports with control towers in the United States. For the calendar year 1964, there were 124,938 operations — planes landing and departing — logged at Smith Reynolds. These included private and charter flights, as well as commercial schedules. Thus, while Smith Reynolds has the service of only one commercial airline, it has a heavy flow of private air travel by businesses and industries in the area. This is a further indication of the community's important stake in the airport.

There were 57,107 airline passengers through the airport in 1965, and 55,984 passengers were recorded in the first nine months of 1966.

In a survey report in March, 1963, Graham reported to the Forsyth County Airport Commission that general aviation flights brought slightly more than one million dollars annually into the area. "The survey reveals that 90 per cent of our visitors flew here on business. Sixty per cent traveled by single-engine aircraft and 40 per cent by multi-engine aircraft," the report stated.

Another report from Graham in May, 1964, said the 1,079 persons employed by local airport tenants share an annual payroll of $7,405,607. The figure was developed, Graham explained, through a survey of all companies having airport facilities, requesting the number of employees at the airport and their annual payroll.

The principal tenant, of course, is Piedmont Airlines, which maintains an important repair operation at the airport as well as its commercial flights. Piedmont Airlines' service provides for the community air links with Washington, D.C., New York, and the Southeastern region and, through connecting airlines, with the nation and the world.

An airport commission, appointed by local government, sees to the operation of the airport. It is a facility whose benefits are available to citizens without any tax expenditures, since it is a self-sustaining operation.

Two industrial parks established by the Airport Commission give promise of further development of aviation-oriented industry. Adjacent land, some of it acquired through the aid of the Foundation, is leased to businesses which need the proximity of an airport.

LIGHT ON A HILL IV

THE PATINA OF AGE has not yet settled on the red brick buildings in the green swell of acres on the northwest edge of Winston-Salem. The trees are pliant in the wind, youthful as the students who walk beneath them between Wait Chapel and Reynolda Hall.

Although Wake Forest has been in its new community only since 1956, it is already very much at home. Each class adds to the body of tradition and sentiment attaching to the campus, while the college, its alumni, and Baptist supporters throughout the state keep strong the sense of historical continuity with the namesake village in Wake County where its life began some 130 years ago.

The removal of the college stands as one of the principal accomplishments of the Z. Smith Reynolds Foundation. Under the impetus of the Foundation's support and encouragement, Wake Forest has traveled far more than the 110-mile distance from its home village to the city of Winston-Salem. It has moved to the forefront among institutions of higher education in its region. This advance can be measured by plant and physical facilities, the intellectual resources of its faculty, the capacity for service to its student body and to society. The growth and development stimulated by relocation has brought Wake Forest today to the threshold of university status.

Moving Wake Forest College to Winston-Salem was a logical idea, growing out of the shift of its medical school in 1941. Through an offer from the heirs of the late Bowman Gray, it became the Bowman Gray School of Medicine and used facilities of the Baptist Hospital in Winston-Salem to expand its clinical program.

Dr. Coy Carpenter, dean of the medical school, said the idea to move the college was raised early in 1941 in a conversation with W. N. Reynolds concerning support for the medical school. Mr. Reynolds asked the question, Dr. Carpenter said, whether the school of medicine would not be stronger "if it were an integral part of a University rather than of a college located 110 miles away."

The late C. J. Jackson, a Wake Forest alumnus who was engaged in raising funds for an enlargement program at the college, reported that in the spring of 1945 the possibility of Winston-Salem as a new home for the college "was discussed in confidence with a few sympathetic friends in Winston-Salem and Charlotte."

L. D. Long, a Foundation trustee and close associate of W. N. Reynolds, said his first recollection was a joking reference he made to Dr. Carpenter. "I told him they already had the medical school here; they should bring over the rest of the college, too," said Long. "He seemed to think that was a pretty good idea." Whether begun in jest or earnest, the removal idea struck sparks at a luncheon on July 16, 1945, in Winston-Salem. Those present included Dr. Carpenter, Long, and Gordon Gray, Winston-Salem publisher and son of the late Bowman Gray.

Following the luncheon, Gray called on W. N. Reynolds to discuss the idea.

Mr. and Mrs. Charles H. Babcock, also Foundation trustees,

Wait Chapel on the campus of Wake Forest College

later were drawn into the discussions. They also were enthusiastic. Wheels were in motion.

Several factors made the project appealing to the Foundation trustees. For one, it represented an opportunity to develop higher education in the northwestern region. Approximately three-quarters of North Carolina's population lived west of Raleigh, but four major institutions of higher learning were grouped within thirty miles of the state capitol—Wake Forest, Duke University at Durham, the University of North Carolina at Chapel Hill, and North Carolina State College at Raleigh.

The Foundation could eventually have built a university from scratch at Winston-Salem. The trustees realized this, but they sensed the advantages to be gained from aiding an existing institution. By calling upon the loyalty and support of Baptists, state-wide strength would be assured for the enterprise. Thus, the location of Wake Forest in Winston-Salem would both provide better educational opportunity for youth of the region and enhance the higher educational resources for the whole state.

From the beginning, W. N. Reynolds gave unstinted leadership. As president of the trustees, he guided the Foundation's participation. He made personal gifts to the new campus building program. While in his mid-eighties, he actively solicited contributions among his Winston-Salem friends.

Clearly, this was an enterprise to which he attached great importance. He had served many years on the Duke University board of trustees, which gave him the opportunity to observe at close range the transformation of a church-supported college through the philanthropy of a tobacco fortune. It is certain the experience made a strong impression. It may have been a factor in his deep interest in the Wake Forest project, and perhaps it shaped some of the principles set out in the Foundation's agreement with the college.

Important items included in the agreement were that the name of the college should not be changed; that its control should continue unaltered and undiminished in the board of trustees chosen by the Baptist State Convention; that the Baptists of North Carolina, through the convention, should continue at the same level their support of the college.

On its part, the Foundation pledged its income up to $350,000 per year in perpetuity to the college if it should make the move. Actually, at the time the agreement was made, the Foundation's income was only about $235,000 per year. By the time Wake Forest was on the Winston-Salem campus, the Foundation's income had increased. Effective in 1955, the pledge was raised to $500,000 per year in perpetuity.

The offer was first put in written form in a letter, dated February 27, 1946, from W. N. Reynolds to C. J. Jackson. The Foundation trustees already had signified informal acceptance, and their president added:

If this proposal meets with the approval of the College authorities, and the requirements set out are met, with the exceptions referred to, in my opinion, the Trustees of the Smith Reynolds Foundation would formally approve resolutions carrying out the terms of this proposal.

An exchange of correspondence between W. N. Reynolds and Dr. Ralph A. Herring, pastor of the First Baptist Church of Winston-Salem, set the stage for a special meeting of the Board of Trustees of Wake Forest College on March 26, 1946. The trustees created a committee, with former Governor J. M. Broughton as chairman, "to investigate very fully the Reynolds proposal and related matters, such committee to report at a joint meeting of the Board of Trustees of the College and the General Board of the Convention with the Educational Council, to be held at Wake Forest on April 11, 1946." Other members of the committee were Dr. Herring, Judge Johnson J. Hayes, Robert P. Holding, Dr.

Thurman Kitchin, Irving E. Carlyle, Dr. Charles H. Durham, and J. Edward Allen.

The public got its first inkling of the matter on the eve of the March 26 meeting of the trustees. Reaction among the state's 600,000 Baptists was dramatic and varied. Many believed it assured the college's future, but others doubted. *Old Gold and Black,* the campus newspaper, recorded the reception of the news in Wake Forest. "An atomic bomb could not have been more sudden, more unexpected, nor stunning," it said.

After the first shock wore off, the offer received closer scrutiny and a rising level of support. Leaders among Baptist laymen in promoting its acceptance included Broughton; Basil M. Watkins, a Durham attorney; Judge Hayes; and Carlyle, a Winston-Salem attorney. The college's board of trustees accepted the offer. The General Board of the Baptist State Convention gave its assent, and a full session of the convention was called to meet in Greensboro on July 30, 1946.

Actually, the college's trustees had authority to make the decision. They sought the endorsement of the State Convention as a means of marshaling full support within the denomination for the undertaking.

So, the 3,000 messengers from Baptist churches across the state met and listened to a full day of debate on the proposal. Broughton, as chairman of the special committee, presented the resolution to accept the offer. By a tremendous vote—observers estimated 95 to 97 per cent favored it—the Convention gave approval.

A first, vital question was whether the Foundation legally could commit its income, or a portion of it, to a specific project "in perpetuity." Through a friendly suit, the courts were asked to supply the answer. Chief Justice W. P. Stacy wrote the opinion when the State Supreme Court decided the case. It concluded:

THE Z. SMITH REYNOLDS FOUNDATION   39

finally, after all is said and done the case comes to a relatively narrow compass. Is the contract submitted for judication valid and enforceable? The trial court thought it was. We approve. Wake Forest College has had a long and honorable career and whether it nestles in a forest of Wake, or stands on a knoll in Forsyth, its mission will remain a quest for truth and a crusade for simple right. We have not denied to this great institution and to those whose faith and good works have made it possible this vista of a new dawn and this vision of a new hope.

The new dawn, though definite on the horizon, was to be years in coming. Mr. and Mrs. Charles H. Babcock, Foundation trustees, made available 300 acres of their Reynolda estate for the new campus. Still ahead lay the arduous task of acquiring funds and raising buildings in order to make the move a reality.

Here the Foundation also gave a helping hand. Its support for the college was to begin in 1947. Judge Hayes, serving on a committee of Wake Forest trustees involved in the removal project, pointed out that the college could not wisely use the money for purposes of operation while still in the old location. He suggested that the funds be allowed to accumulate for buildings on the new campus. This was done, and eventually it meant some $3,200,000 for the building program.

Meanwhile, a campaign was launched among Baptist churches to raise $1,500,000. The Winston-Salem community began an effort to provide another $1,500,000. Sale of the old campus to the Southern Baptist Convention, for a new seminary, was arranged for $1,600,000.

As these efforts were pushing forward, a change in administration came about for the college. Retirement ended the twenty-year presidency of Dr. Thurman Kitchin. After a diligent search, Dr. Harold W. Tribble was brought in as his successor.

Dr. Tribble took over the reins in September, 1950, and immediately plunged into the removal campaign. In the spring of 1951, a challenge gift campaign was projected, based upon an anonymous offer of $2,000,000 on the condition that Wake Forest should raise $3,000,000 from other sources. Later, the identity of donors of the challenge gift came to light as W. N. Reynolds, who pledged $1,500,000, and Nancy Reynolds Verney, who pledged the remaining $500,000. When W. N. Reynolds died before the conclusion of the campaign, the Z. Smith Reynolds Foundation agreed to take up his share of the challenge offer. The college announced that the matching $3,000,000 had been raised by early in January, 1954, to qualify for the $2,000,000 challenge gift.

To dramatize the college's commitment to move, and to stimulate response to appeals for building funds, ground-breaking ceremonies were planned for the new campus.

President Harry S. Truman, himself a Baptist, came to turn the first spade of earth. "A college is an institution that is dedicated to the future. It is based on faith and hope," he told the crowd assembled at the site on October 15, 1951.

It was an auspicious occasion, marred only by the absence of one who had done much to bring it about. W. N. Reynolds, in his eighty-eighth year, passed away September 10, 1951.

His will left $1,000,000 to Wake Forest for the construction program. In addition, it created a trust of approximately $14,000,000 with income payable to the Z. Smith Reynolds Foundation. In this way, it seemed his intention to give permanence to his promise to continue support for Wake Forest in its new location.

Jens Frederick Larson of New York City, an architect with much experience in college design, chose a style of modified Georgian for the campus. Actual construction began in June, 1952, thus meeting the deadline set out in the agreement with the Z. Smith Reynolds Foundation. Appropriately, the first building to rise was Wait Chapel, the center of religious life for the campus. It

Laying the cornerstone of the Z. Smith Reynolds Library, October 3, 1953. Charles H. Babcock, rear; Richard J. Reynolds, standing; and Stratton Coyner, back to camera

was named for Samuel Wait, minister and the college's first president.

Four years remained before Wake Forest set up permanent housekeeping in Winston-Salem. Fund-raising drives continued unabated. The Korean conflict intervened. Resulting material shortages hampered construction and pushed prices upward. Fresh difficulties called for renewed efforts to overcome them. Finally, in the fall of 1956, came the dedication of the campus.

The college, the community, and the Foundation joined in rejoicing; indeed, the whole state and the academic world beyond the state took part in celebrating the consummation of a significant educational enterprise.

A highlight of the dedication ceremonies was the presentation by Dr. Tribble, Wake Forest president, of a scroll of appreciation to the Z. Smith Reynolds Foundation trustees. The inscription declared: "Through their wisdom and leadership, emphasizing fruitful continuity with the past and stimulating new interest and generosity in others, these Trustees have become, in a real sense, the founders of the new Wake Forest."

In accepting the scroll, Richard J. Reynolds, Jr., president of the trustees, replied: "The Foundation's part was more like striking a match to light a fire. I certainly want to recognize the thousands of good Baptists who have contributed so greatly to make the new Wake Forest become a reality."

Wake Forest today is a demonstrably stronger institution, academically as well as in material resources, than it had prospects of becoming in its original location.

One of the essential measures of a college is its faculty and the degrees its faculty members hold. In this regard, upgrading at Wake Forest has been little short of startling. For the 1946–47 academic year, twenty members of the undergraduate faculty held Ph.D. degrees. This represented 41.67 per cent of the faculty. For the 1966–67 year, 125 undergraduate faculty members, or 70.22 per cent, held the Ph.D. degree. Incidentally, over this period the undergraduate faculty increased from 48 to 178.

Faculty salaries is another barometer of a college's standing. It is a natural consequence that the college with attractive salary schedules draws faculty of talent and ability. These figures show

THE Z. SMITH REYNOLDS FOUNDATION   43

how the Wake Forest undergraduate faculty has fared from 1946 to 1966, with the salary for the earlier year listed first: professor $4,200 and $9,500–$16,000; associate professor $3,750 and $9,000–$11,200; assistant professor $3,000–$3,500 and $7,500–$10,500; instructor $1,500–$2,400 and $5,400–$8,500.

Student enrollment has gone from about 1,700 for the 1946 fall term to 3,022 in the fall of 1966. An even more dramatic growth has been shown in summer school enrollment, which was 867 in 1946 and reached slightly over 1,900 in 1966.

In view of the progress made, the Z. Smith Reynolds Foundation in 1962 made available a $30,000 grant for a study by Dr. Roger P. McCutcheon and Dr. Oliver Carmichael of the college's graduate program, looking towards its further development. Among other things, the study indicated a need to build up library resources as one step in strengthening graduate studies at Wake Forest.

The study grant was evidence of the Foundation's continuing interest in the development of Wake Forest, and illustrated the dynamic nature of the agreement between the college and the Foundation. Neither party has regarded the contract as a restrictive instrument, but rather as a guide. Both readily agree that the other has far exceeded the minimum requirements set out in the contract.

North Carolina Baptists have made it amply clear that they recognize a continuing responsibility for the support of Wake Forest College, as W. N. Reynolds contemplated they would. The agreement with the Foundation called for support by the Baptist State Convention on a level at least equal to that provided for the college in 1946. Under the accepted formula, this called for the college to receive at least 7.5 per cent of the Convention's distributable income. In no year since that time has the Convention failed to exceed its obligation by a substantial margin.

Wake Forest College campus.   Z. Smith Reynolds Library in background

In dollars, this has meant that Convention support for the college has increased from $78,200 in 1946 to $350,099 in 1966. Using the 7.5 per cent formula, the college was due $306,956 of the Convention's 1966 distributable income of $4,092,742. The amount it received exceeded this by $43,143.

Through December 31, 1966, the Foundation's support for Wake Forest, exclusive of scholarships and other help for the Bowman Gray School of Medicine, had amounted to $11,031,253. All of this has been given without any attempt to dictate the policy to the college, or to interfere in any manner with its operation.

"Faculty members and those in college administration feel very jealous about academic freedom," a professor remarked. "Unquestionably, the hands-off attitude of the Foundation and its trustees has been the basis for the strong mutual respect."

PLAYGROUND FOR A REGION   V

TANGLEWOOD IS AN APT, EXPRESSIVE NAME. Something about the untrammeled forest invites relaxation, an easing of tensions. Here, the forest is always present. It is seen from the cultivated roll of the golf course and from the fenced enclosure of the swimming pool.

There are two stories to explain how the name came to be applied to the picturesque area along the Yadkin River, near Clemmons, N.C., which is a playground for people from Winston-Salem, Forsyth County, a widening region of Piedmont North Carolina, and beyond.

The first says it came from Nathaniel Hawthorne's *Tanglewood Tales.* Certainly, the landscape is romantic enough to have inspired such a choice.

The second says a visiting industrialist provided the name with the matter-of-fact comment, while looking over the site, "It is a tangled wood."

Whatever the origin, it was Kate B. Reynolds who gave the name to the property, and it has remained firmly and appropriately attached.

The more formal name now is "The William and Kate B. Reynolds Memorial Park." Mr. and Mrs. Reynolds, by will, created the park from their estate and homeplace, leaving for follow-

ing generations to enjoy what during their lifetimes had given them, and their frequent guests, so much pleasure. Their generosity made Tanglewood something unique: a recreation center wholly supported by private funds for public benefit rather than commercial profit.

Many, many persons enjoyed the gracious hospitality of Tanglewood with Mr. and Mrs. Reynolds as hosts; uncounted others now follow each season, using the park's facilities for varied entertainment in nature's beautiful setting.

Over the park's first decade, the Z. Smith Reynolds Foundation contributed $1,010,300 to its development. The Foundation's interest sprang naturally from its close ties with W. N. Reynolds, who helped guide its beginning, served as trustee and president, and greatly enriched its resources through a trust with income payable to the Foundation. Two of the Foundation's trustees, L. D. Long and William R. Lybrook, also serve as trustees for the park under the wills of W. N. Reynolds and his wife. Long is a trustee under both wills, and Lybrook is a trustee under the W. N. Reynolds will only.

The Mary Reynolds Babcock Foundation, formed from the estate of one of the founders of the Z. Smith Reynolds Foundation, also has been a principal contributor of capital funds for the park. Others who have aided have included the Container Corporation of America, the Duke Power Company, the Duplan Corporation, the Hanes Dye and Finishing Company, the Hanes Hosiery Mills Company, the John W. and Anna Hodgin Hanes Foundation, the P. H. Hanes Knitting Company, the Kate B. Reynolds Trust, the R. J. Reynolds Tobacco Company, the Security Life and Trust Company, Slick Enterprises, the Wachovia Bank & Trust Company, the North Carolina National Bank, and others. So, in a real sense, development of the park has involved many persons and organizations and has reflected a community's high regard for the couple whose memorial it is.

Though its woodlands keep an uncultivated air, Tanglewood's growth has not been haphazard. The pattern was drawn by F. Ellwood Allen of Bennington, Vermont, perhaps the country's top professional in park planning. Allen keeps an eye on progress along the path he has laid out, visiting the park twice a year or so, conferring with park officials to explore ideas for future development.

Looking back over the first ten years of operation, Allen wrote in 1964:

Ten years ago, Tanglewood Park was a diamond in the rough; a dream, but a dream without a flaw. Today it is a dramatic reality, with its coruscating facets beaming light into the lives of hundreds of people. It is a living tribute to those men of courage and vision who never lost faith in its destiny and to the many, humble and affluent, who gave so unsparingly in labor and love to make this memorial what it is today.

The beginning might be dated 1921, when W. N. Reynolds purchased from Thomas W. Griffith the property which formed the nucleus for what was to become Tanglewood Park. It was a storied area, embracing the square mile that was bought by William Johnson in 1757 from Lord Granville, one of the Lords Proprietors of the colony of North Carolina. It is said he paid 80 pounds sterling. Skirmishes in the French and Indian War led Johnson to build a fort overlooking the Yadkin River for protection. Today, the hardy Welsh immigrant sleeps quietly in an ancient graveyard within the park.

W. N. Reynolds loved horses. He bred and trained trotters and pacers. Soon Tanglewood Farm was famous as the home of Stand-

An early morning view across the Manor House lawn at Tanglewood

ardbred horses, and such racing notables as "Tarheel" and "Solicitor." Mrs. Reynolds lavished her attention on roses and the grounds of the mid-nineteenth-century Manor House which they had restored as their home.

They added to Tanglewood until it encompassed just over 1,100 acres. Together they decided they wished it to have a continuing future. Their wills left the estate as a park and provided 20,000 shares (now 80,000 because of splits) of R. J. Reynolds Tobacco Co. stock as a permanent endowment, plus approximately $200,000 for initial development. Following Mr. Reynolds' death in September, 1951 (his wife had died five years earlier), the trustees named in the wills acted to bring the park into being. In addition to Long and Lybrook, the trustees are John C. Whitaker and the Wachovia Bank & Trust Company.

The trustees consulted officials of the National Park Service, the North Carolina State Parks Division, and the Winston-Salem City Recreation Department. It was at this time that the decision was made to employ Allen to create the plan for developing the park.

With only basic facilities, the park swung open its gates in June, 1954. There were lakes for boating and fishing, trails for horseback riding and a stable, campgrounds and picnic areas, the beginning of an arboretum, and a six-acre deer park.

There was also Mt. Pleasant Methodist Church, a simple, sturdy frame structure built in 1809. Restored by Senah Critz Kent, a niece of W. N. Reynolds, the church gives visitors a calm atmosphere for meditation as well as a commanding view of the surrounding countryside. Summer vesper services are held there on Sunday evenings, as well as an occasional wedding or other gathering.

The swimming pool and the golf course have been the principal projects supported by the Z. Smith Reynolds Foundation. Its first grant to the park was $175,000 approved by the trustees in 1953 for swimming pool construction. A supplementary amount of $78,300 for the same purpose was provided in 1955.

Early development of the park was guided by a management group consisting of trustees and leading local citizens with R. Murray Lybrook as park superintendent. He had been farm manager for W. N. Reynolds, and he brought to the post of superintendent not only a thorough familiarity with the property but also a keen business sense and a penetrating insight into the problems of park development. His untimely death in 1957 was a real loss to the park. Camp Murray Lybrook, which offers a camping program for boys, perpetuates his association with the park. Boys earn their camp tuition by working at park jobs, thus gaining a wholesome experience they could not otherwise afford.

Gardner Gidley succeeded Murray Lybrook, and efficient management continued as a major factor in the park's development. Gidley resigned in the summer of 1965 and was followed by Marlin Roger Warren as park general manager. Warren, a graduate of Wake Forest College, had been on the Tanglewood staff since 1958, as recreation director and assistant manager.

Construction of a golf course was authorized in 1956, and the Z. Smith Reynolds Foundation made available $100,000 to get the work started. Robert Trent Jones was retained to design the championship course. Other grants of $175,000 in 1957 and $70,000 in 1958 completed the 18-hole course.

The Foundation in 1963 contributed $100,000 towards a 9-hole addition to the golf course.

The other major park project supported by the Z. Smith Reynolds Foundation has been the remodeling of the Manor House to provide dining and lodging facilities. A $200,000 grant for the purpose was provided in 1959.

The deer park at Tanglewood

Tanglewood has attracted an increasing number of visitors each year. As its popularity has grown, the park has become more and more a self-sustaining operation.

As the park's popularity has grown, its visitors have come from a wider region. Officials estimate that perhaps 50 per cent of park use represents Winston-Salem and Forsyth County people, 35 per cent North Carolina citizens, and 15 per cent tourists and visitors from other states and areas.

The Civil Rights Act of 1964 posed serious questions for Tanglewood. The wills of W. N. and Kate B. Reynolds specified use of the park by white citizens. The trustees under the wills went to the court for instructions. They were satisfied, as a result of the judicial decision, that operation of Tanglewood should continue, under the terms of the wills, as long as programs did not conflict with the federal act.

As a result, some activities were eliminated. Renewed emphasis was given to camping, family picnicking, and related park uses. The trustees promised their best efforts to find new programs for those displaced by changing times.

Like nature, constantly renewing herself for fresh generations, Tanglewood keeps a continuing legacy for those fortunate enough to find its refuge.

LAMPS FOR LEARNING VI

SENTIMENT AND VISION might be said to be the distinguishing marks of the Z. Smith Reynolds Foundation's scholarship programs. The trustees have first looked close at home in giving aid to students in need. Once goals were fixed, they have displayed rare insight in moving directly to meet them.

Continuing scholarship programs now occupy an important place in the Foundation's schedule of activity and account for more than $300,000 in annual grants. There are four principal groups: the Reynolds Medical Scholarships, Bowman Gray School of Medicine, Wake Forest College; the Katharine Smith Reynolds Scholarships for young women, University of North Carolina at Greensboro; the Nancy Jane Cox Reynolds Scholarships for graduates of Stokes County high schools; and the Z. Smith Reynolds Foundation Scholarships for Negro youth attending Bennett, Livingstone, and other colleges.

In addition, the Foundation has supported scholarship awards at Winston-Salem State College and North Carolina College at Durham.

Scholarships are an intensely personal form of philanthropy. Aid is given directly to a specific student, who forms a relationship with the giver. If his academic career is successful, he will carry the scholarship identification throughout life. In this manner, for example, the Foundation has earned wide respect in the medical profession because of the scholarships at Bowman Gray.

The Z. Smith Reynolds Foundation came to scholarships as a secondary line of activity. Its initial efforts dealt with social issues in the large: combatting a disease that ravaged segments of society, and developing an educational institution to serve a broad area of the state and region.

It was not until 1952 that the Foundation entered the area of awards to individual students by taking over the W. N. Reynolds prizes to outstanding students at Winston-Salem State College. "Mr. Will" Reynolds had established the awards, and following his death the Foundation continued them in his name with a $500 grant for prizes totaling $100 annually over a period of five years. These were not, strictly speaking, scholarships but prizes for scholastic achievement. However, they marked a beginning.

The Nancy Jane Cox Reynolds Memorial School in Stokes County, named in honor of the grandmother of the founders of the Z. Smith Reynolds Foundation, received aid from the Foundaation first in 1956. A grant of $35,000 was approved, on recommendation of a committee of William R. Lybrook and L. D. Long, for the construction and equipment of a vocational and agricultural building. The trustees' minutes noted Lybrook's report that "resources of this community were such that few of the high school graduates went to college." For this reason, he said, the vocational and agricultural courses would be particularly helpful.

The school is located in an area of Stokes County where the Reynoldses have close ties of ancestry. Lack of educational opportunities in a community so touched with family sentiment evidently continued to concern the trustees. Two years later, they decided to do something about giving graduates of the Nancy Jane Cox Reynolds School a chance to go to college. They made available $6,000 to the Stokes County Board of Education for the selection of three graduates to receive scholarships of $500 per year for four years.

This was continued as an annual program until 1964, when changes were made to take into account school consolidations in Stokes County. The Foundation named the awards the Nancy Jane Cox Reynolds Memorial Scholarships and broadened eligibility to include graduates of all three high schools in the county. The annual amount of the scholarships was raised from $500 to $1,000 each, taking into account the increased cost of college study.

The new arrangement provides a $12,000 annual grant for three scholarships of $1,000 each, for four years, selection being made by the county board of education. In the event a scholarship holder drops out of college, the remainder of the award can be used for another student.

The medical scholarships at the Bowman Gray School of Medicine came into being on November 26, 1957, when the trustees adopted the resolution for their establishment. This launched a $150,000 per year project, supporting eight four-year scholarships annually. These are among the most liberal scholarships available for medical study, and their purpose is to attract bright young North Carolinians into the field of medicine. A condition of the scholarships is an agreement that the recipient will practice five years in North Carolina, although this is waived if the scholar enters teaching or research, or otherwise is unable to keep it.

Dr. Coy Carpenter, vice-president for medical affairs at Wake Forest College, candidly calls the scholarship program "one of the greatest things that ever happened to our medical school. It has given us national prestige. It has enabled us to attract the best young brains in North Carolina to come to our school, including some particularly bright young people who needed and could receive one of those scholarships."

The program was one proposed to the school by Richard J. Reynolds, Jr., Dr. Carpenter recalled. "It was not solicited by us. He came to us with the idea," the medical school head pointed out. It was Reynolds' feeling that young men and women who chose medicine were penalized, in effect, by the long period of study required. He wanted to set up scholarships liberal enough so that the medical student need not give up marriage and a family, for example, until the completion of his education.

"I really tried to persuade him to distribute these things widely because I knew there was so much need," said Dr. Carpenter. "But he insisted he wanted these scholarship grants to go to boys and girls coming to our medical school from North Carolina, with enough money so that they might be even with young people going into fields requiring less extensive preparation."

In addition to the scholarship fund, an annual grant of $5,000 goes to the Bowman Gray School of Medicine for the Richard J. Reynolds Lectureship Program. This brings distinguished visiting professors to the campus. One of these visitors is the speaker for the annual awards dinner, when a $1,000 prize goes to the outstanding senior Reynolds scholar.

These requirements are laid down for the winner:

His character, personality and academic standing should be such that he is potentially a doctor of the highest quality. His academic standing should be high but need not be the highest among the Reynolds scholars. He should possess warmth of feeling for his fellow men. He should have the ability to inspire confidence.

In addition to scholarship aid, each Reynolds scholar as an intern receives a supplementary payment from the Foundation. This is an amount sufficient, when added to the salary from the institution where internship is served, to total $5,000 annually.

The Admissions Committee of the school selects scholarship winners, on the basis of ability and need. The awards are presented at a dinner bringing together candidates, school officials, and trustees of the Z. Smith Reynolds Foundation. Wives and husbands also attend, for an affair which has the warmth of a social occasion as well as a seriousness of purpose.

The Foundation's willingness to bend to meet special circumstances was illustrated by the situation of Hugh and Van Noah, twin brothers of Raleigh, N.C., with almost identical scholastic records. When they applied for Reynolds Medical Scholarships, the trustees accepted the solution, of splitting a single scholarship between the brothers. While the trustees acknowledged that this seemed the best way to handle the twins' case, they specified that it should not be taken as a precedent for splitting the scholarships.

The eight scholarships carry the following designations, with each scholar receiving his checks directly, marked by the appropriate title:

The Mary Reynolds Babcock Scholarship
The William Neal Reynolds Scholarship
The Nancy Reynolds Verney Scholarship
The Richard J. Reynolds Scholarship
The Robert Edward Lasater Scholarship
The Nancy Lybrook Lasater Scholarship
The Walter R. Reynolds Scholarship
The Lucy Reynolds Critz Scholarship

The Katharine Smith Reynolds Scholarships were established on November 16, 1962, when the trustees of the Z. Smith Reynolds Foundation adopted the program to aid young women seeking a college education. The scholarships honor the mother of Z. Smith Reynolds and provide for study at her alma mater. At the time of their creation, the University of North Carolina at Greensboro was known as the Woman's College of the University of North Carolina and normally restricted enrollment to women students.

Three young women at the University of North Carolina at Greensboro studying under Katharine Smith Reynolds Scholarships

Financed by annual grants of $57,600, the scholarships provide for the selection of twelve young women each year to receive $1,200 annual grants, renewable for four years' study. Thus, at the end of four years, a total of forty-eight Katharine Smith Reynolds scholars are on campus, and the number will be maintained at that level.

Eleven of the candidates are chosen from eleven districts of the state. The twelfth scholarship provides for study in chemistry for a young woman from the county of Surry, Stokes, or Forsyth. District committees composed of alumnae of the school make nominations to a Central Scholarship Committee.

The young women to receive scholarships are chosen on the basis of scholastic ability, financial need, and "evidence of moral force of character including truthfulness, courage, devotion to duty, unselfishness, and consideration for others."

Anne Reynolds Forsyth, a granddaughter of Katharine Smith Reynolds, serves as the Foundation's representative on the Central Scholarship Committee. Faculty members and alumnae representatives make up the remainder of the committee membership.

A third substantial scholarship program was set up by the Foundation in the fall of 1964, envisioning broader opportunities in higher education for Negro youth in North Carolina. A grant of $100,000 made available $1,000-per-year awards to twenty-four students. Nine young women were chosen to attend Bennett College in Greensboro; nine young men were selected to attend Livingstone College in Salisbury; another six scholarships were awarded to qualified Negro students who were finalists in the National Achievement Scholarship Program, for attendance at the colleges of their choice. The remaining $4,000 went to the colleges for administration of the scholarships.

The first of the Z. Smith Reynolds Foundation scholarships were awarded for study beginning in the fall of 1965. Another $100,000 grant was authorized, under which twenty-four additional scholars began study in the fall of 1966.

Recipients of the scholarships were chosen by a steering committee composed of John Wheeler, president of Mechanics and Farmers Bank, Durham, chairman; Mrs. Martin L. Cannon, Jr., Charlotte; Dr. Hollis Edens, executive director of the Mary Reynolds Babcock Foundation, Winston-Salem; Dr. Sam Duncan, president of Livingstone College, Salisbury; and Dr. Willa B. Player, president of Bennett College, Greensboro. The selection of scholarship winners was guided by "financial need, scholastic ability, and character of the applicants, as well as geographic distribution. . . ." While the aim was to spread the scholarships across the state, no quotas or limits were set by areas.

The Z. Smith Reynolds Foundation scholarships represented a logical development in aid to Negro education, which began, in a sense, with the taking over of the W. N. Reynolds awards at Winston-Salem State College.

The Foundation has supported academic improvement at Winston-Salem State College through scholarships for faculty members to enable them to pursue graduate study. The first of these received approval in 1958, when $15,000 was granted for three scholarships of $5,000 each. Recipients were selected by the executive committee of the college's academic accreditation committee.

A similar, but increased, grant was made in 1962, when $25,000 was provided for five scholarships of $5,000 each, payable over a three-year period.

Another grant in the area of Negro education was made in 1961, when $4,000 was turned over to the James E. Shepard Memorial Foundation, Inc., for scholarships to incoming freshmen at North Carolina College in Durham.

ADVENTURE IN PARTNERSHIP VII

COMPLEXITIES OF HIGHER EDUCATION TODAY have opened up a vital area of partnership for the private foundation and the tax-supported institution. The relationship of the Z. Smith Reynolds Foundation and North Carolina State University, Raleigh, well illustrates the point.

The state has the responsibility to provide opportunities for higher education for the rapidly increasing number of young people. It is under obligation to spend its tax dollars carefully, concentrating on basic programs of study. The private foundation, on the other hand, may provide the incentive for an enrichment of the program and facilities with the assurance of a maximum benefit to the state or region. Often the foundation can give the funds, unavailable from any other source, which serve as a lever which the state-supported institution can use to accomplish even greater goals.

A natural basis existed for the Z. Smith Reynolds Foundation's interest in N.C. State, a unit of the Consolidated University of North Carolina. As a center for agricultural study, the campus is the site for scientific research involving tobacco. This is an activity of direct concern to a large segment of the population of North Carolina.

Also, N.C. State was the alma mater of Richard J. Reynolds, Jr. Throughout his life, he kept a keen interest in its welfare.

Three projects at N.C. State have been sponsored by the Z. Smith Reynolds Foundation:

Alumni Association Building, 1958, renovation and furnishing, $100,000.

Faculty Recreation Center, 1959–61, total of $800,000.

Phytotron, plant research facility, $750,000 grant authorized in 1962.

While the Alumni Building aid might appear in the light of a dutiful alumnus' contribution, the Foundation took care to see that its investment would continue to pay dividends. This is the condition for the $100,000 gift, stipulated in the minutes of the Foundation:

provided that the North Carolina State College Alumni Association, Inc. will then agree to provide each year in perpetuity, beginning in the fall of 1959, the sum of $3,000 to support a minimum of six scholarships in the amount of $500 each to be awarded to well qualified applicants to be selected in the same manner and upon the same terms and conditions as are followed and used in selecting those to be awarded that are now known as the "Talent for Service" Scholarships. The scholarships, thus to be established are to be named in honor of Richard J. Reynolds.

Thus, it might be said the Foundation assured a 3 per cent return on its grant, with the beneficiaries to be young North Carolinians in search of an education.

The Foundation's trustees showed an imaginative grasp of unorthodox ways to aid higher education when they approved plans for a Faculty Club at N.C. State. Nancy Reynolds Verney, who served on the committee which planned the center, said the idea was that pleasant living circumstances would be an important factor in recruiting and keeping a competent academic staff. "Indirectly, the college might be able to get instruction of better quality through the fact that the faculty and their families were happier in the community," she explained.

The recollection on the N.C. State campus is that the Faculty Club had its genesis during a visit by Richard J. Reynolds, Jr., then Foundation president. Reynolds was shown the handsome new Erdahl-Cloyd Student Union. "This is for our students, to spend their leisure time," college officials said proudly.

"What about your faculty?" asked Reynolds. "What kind of facilities do they have?"

After a moment of surprised silence, his hosts had to reply that there was nothing comparable for faculty members.

The first grant of $500,000 for the project was made by the Foundation on December 2, 1959. This provided that the North Carolina State College Foundation, Inc., would acquire land for the center, which would be constructed, furnished, and turned over for use by the college faculty. The late Leroy Martin, Raleigh banker, was named to serve with Reynolds and his sister Mrs. Verney on a committee to employ an architect and proceed with plans. A second grant of $300,000 was approved on December 15, 1961, for the completion of the center.

Located on rolling land lying on Raleigh's western outskirts, a brief drive from the campus, the center has more than lived up to expectations. It has quickly become a rallying point for the campus' social and professional life. Equally important, it has given the institution an appropriate setting for meeting civic and business leaders from the community and beyond.

"The Faculty Club is a much appreciated and valuable thing—a unifying force, a morale builder," said Chancellor John T. Caldwell. "Few people in an academic community have the opportunity to belong to a country club. This fills that lack, and with a quality facility which adds tremendously to the faculty's sense of belonging to a first-class institution."

Visiting dignitaries and delegations get at least one meal at the

The Faculty Club at North Carolina State University, Raleigh

club. They are impressed, Dr. Caldwell noted. "They all say, 'We wish we had something like this. How did you get it?' and we don't miss the opportunity to tell them." The Foundation's role also is cited on a plaque in the club lobby.

Dr. Brooks James, dean of the life sciences division, feels there is no doubt the club aids in recruitment. "We don't bring anyone here for an interview without at least one stop at the club," he said. "It represents an important fringe benefit which means a lot to a faculty prospect and his family."

Through monthly dues, faculty members provide for themselves the use of facilities such as a dining room; a nine-hole, par-three golf course; a swimming pool; and tennis courts.

The Faculty Center is an example of the cooperation of a private foundation with a tax-supported institution to make available a facility that would have been difficult to provide from ordinary sources of support.

The phytotron project demonstrates a further step in private-public partnership.

First, it should be explained that a phytotron is a research facility that permits study of plants under a variety of conditions as to humidity, light, and temperature. The use of an integrated group of controlled environment rooms and cabinets permits scientists, in effect, to reproduce any kind of environment and study the plant's reaction. There has been world-wide interest in phytotrons among plant scientists over the past two decades. At present, four large ones are in operation. These are located at Pasadena, California; Gif, France; Moscow, Russia; and Canberra, Australia. There has been a recognized need for additional facilities in this country.

The Reynolds Foundation, on April 30, 1962, approved a $750,000 grant for a phytotron at N.C. State. Soon after, the college learned that Duke University in Durham was interested in a National Science Foundation grant for a phytotron for its campus. Should a public and a private institution duplicate facilities within thirty miles of each other? Should one step aside in favor of the other? Talks were set in motion between the two campuses to make a decision.

The result was a cooperative proposal for a two-unit regional phytotron. One unit would be located on each campus. A coordinating board would include representation from each institution. The National Science Foundation accepted the idea and awarded $1,250,000 to Duke and $1,000,000 to N.C. State to supplement the Reynolds Foundation grant.

Scientists are excited at the prospect. Dr. R. J. Downs, phytotron director for the N.C. State unit, said it will be a unique facility which will greatly expand research opportunities for the two campuses involved, and for the region.

The phytotron at N.C. State will be housed in its own building, an annex to Gardner Hall. However, Dean Brooks James pointed out that such a project requires "a great deal of engineering, and there is not a lot to pattern after." Recent reports indicate the facility should be operational in 1967.

Chancellor Caldwell looks forward to the phytotron as a strengthening of N.C. State's role in pushing back the frontiers of knowledge. "Man must know much more about environment's effect upon plants and the disease organisms which attack plants," he explained. "This wonderful tool—and that is what phytotron means, plant tool—will make us far more efficient in our study of plants."

He considers the Reynolds Foundation grant the key to the joint enterprise, involving the National Science Foundation, Duke, and N.C. State. "There is a good chance neither would have gotten a two-unit facility at all if it hadn't been for the Reynolds Foundation grant," he said. "It proved to be a lever for getting a whole lot more. It is a significant example of working together, with private and public sources, to achieve the maximum potential."

IN QUEST OF EXCELLENCE VIII

HIGHER EDUCATION in the years since World War II has felt varied and intense pressures. It has been a time of tremendously expanding knowledge, of revolutionized techniques and equipment for teaching, and of dramatic increase in student population. Simplified, the pressures have come from two directions: for quantity, to extend college-level training to as many as possible in the eligible age bracket; for quality, to strive for higher standards of excellence in academic instruction.

The Z. Smith Reynolds Foundation has been aware of both these currents, in its active programs to improve higher education in North Carolina. It has aided newly established colleges, provided scholarships, and otherwise worked to see that more and more Tar Heel young people have opportunities for education beyond high school. At the same time, it has used its influence for lifting the quality of education, through endowed professorships, aid for libraries, and in other ways.

A striking example of the Foundation's encouragement of excellence is its endowment plan for Davidson College. The Foundation has proposed to make grants to the college over a period of years, until a total of $5,000,000 has been reached. This would make Davidson second only to Wake Forest among educational institutions aided by the Foundation.

The campus of Davidson College

Sound scholarship is a part of the Davidson College tradition. It was founded by Scotch Presbyterians of Piedmont Carolina, and opened its doors on March 1, 1837, charged to "educate youth of all classes without regard to the distinction of religious denominations, thereby to promote the more general diffusion of knowledge and virtue."

To its rural setting on an 80-acre tract, twenty miles north of Charlotte, the college draws students from all over the United States and abroad. Its alumni go on to positions of leadership and service. For example, Davidson ranks in the upper 3 per cent of all private colleges and universities in the percentage of its graduates listed in *Who's Who in America.*

As an indication of its academic excellence, Davidson has had graduates win fifteen Rhodes Scholarships, eight since 1950. This ranks it sixth among the nation's liberal arts colleges in Rhodes Scholars. A recent study showed that Davidson has produced more Ph.D. college professors than any other college in the South.

The quality-quantity dilemma was posed for Davidson in the wake of World War II, as veterans crowded into colleges. "We had a tremendous surge of enrollment, going up from 640 to 1,000," President David Grier Martin recalled. "Obviously, this resulted in a much lower level of academic program than we would have liked to have. When we got over that hump, and enrollment came back to around 860, we instituted a committee representing the faculty, the administration, and the trustees to determine just what Davidson's future should be."

The committee decided for quality. It recommended increasing the enrollment to 1,000 men as soon as qualified teachers and students, adequate physical facilities, and necessary financial resources could be provided, with the goal of the best possible program of liberal arts instruction for a student body of that size.

This requires a careful process of selection for students seeking entrance. Only 265 freshmen can be enrolled; approximately 1,114 completed applications for entrance were received in 1966. Of those finally selected, more than 75 per cent came from the upper 10 per cent of their high school graduating classes, with average college board scores above 600 on both Verbal and Mathematics. They included twenty-five student body presidents, forty-two class presidents, fifteen editors of school papers, forty-three Eagle Scouts, and twenty-eight captains of varsity athletic teams.

The trustees of the Z. Smith Reynolds Foundation on December 2, 1959, approved a grant of $450,000 to establish the Reynolds Distinguished Professorships at Davidson, in honor of Mary Reynolds Babcock and Virginia Lasater Irvin. Charles H. Babcock, Anne Reynolds Forsyth, and Richard J. Reynolds, Jr., were named as a committee of trustees to confer with Davidson officials.

Dr. William P. Cumming holds the Virginia Lasater Irvin Professorship of English, and Dr. J. Alexander McGeachy, Jr., is the Mary Reynolds Babcock Professor of History.

Out of the discussions between trustees and college officials came a decision to use $100,000 of the grant to create the Richard J. Reynolds, Jr., Distinguished Lectureship Fund. The purpose would be to bring to Davidson world leaders in thought for dialogue with students and faculty, thus enriching and stimulating the learning process. To read Arnold Toynbee's *Study of History* is one kind of experience; to hear and question the author is a far more dynamic encounter. Davidson students had the opportunity to hear Toynbee, who came to the campus as a result of the lectureship fund.

"The impact of the Reynolds Distinguished Lectureships in a place like Davidson has been all out of proportion to the cost," said Dr. Martin. "It has brought to this campus distinguished people from all over the world who could not have been attracted here otherwise."

The lecturer spends the better part of two days on campus. "Our students have a chance to really get at him and to pick his mind . . . it is one of the most meaningful experiences we have here," the president continued. "It is particularly important because of our location. We are a sort of rural institution, although we have immediate accessibility to Charlotte. Basically, we have to bring things here, and this program brings them. Not only do students and faculty benefit, but the surrounding community as well. We fill our auditorium with people from within a range of 150 miles."

Lecturers have included Archibald MacLeish, poet, playwright, and scholar; Arnold J. Toynbee, British historian; Dr. Harlow Shapley, astronomer; Dr. Paul Tillich, theologian; Secretary of State Dean Rusk (a Davidson alumnus); Ralph E. McGill, journalist and editor; Mark Van Doren, poet and teacher; George Buttrick, theologian and teacher; and others.

In 1964–65, Davidson trustees endorsed a long-term plan of development with a goal of $25,300,000 in gifts to be raised for plant and endowment purposes by 1975. An important milestone in the campaign came in 1964 when the Z. Smith Reynolds Foundation announced its intention to provide $5,000,000 over a period of years.

"This magnificent series of proposed grants will be the second-largest in Davidson's history," said Dr. Martin. "Davidson still needs a minimum of $17,300,000 by 1975 to achieve the goals established for the college. The grants from the Z. Smith Reynolds Foundation will, I am sure, encourage Davidson alumni, parents, and friends to support as never before the financial needs of this institution."

The quest for academic excellence calls for rich resources in books and men—students, faculty, and library. These are areas for concentration for Davidson's future: wise selection for those seeking entrance, proven ability for those who teach, and the wealth of knowledge in books and other learning resources to undergird the total educational process.

BREAD ON THE WATER IX

SENSITIVITY TO GRASSROOTS needs has spread the influence of the Z. Smith Reynolds Foundation into every corner of North Carolina. Its trustees have sponsored bold programs to serve the whole state, but they have also remained attentive to modest requests for help in specific communities.

With a multitude of grants ranging downward to a few thousand dollars, the Foundation has touched directly more than half of the one hundred counties of the state. Its reach has extended from Southport, in the southeastern coastal corner, to Andrews in the mountainous southwest. Principal beneficiaries have been hospitals, schools and colleges, public libraries, and some special causes.

How widespread Foundation activity has been is seen in the list of individual grants in Appendix IV. It is far too lengthy to treat here, each item in detail. The purpose here, rather, is to survey the broad outlines of the Foundation's work at the local level.

The flexibility represented here is no happy accident, but a definite part of the Foundation's philosophy. Rather than commit its total income to several fixed interests, it has chosen a mixed pattern of action. There are important continuing obligations; the $500,000 annually "in perpetuity" for Wake Forest College is an example. At the same time, the Foundation purposely keeps available a portion of its funds to meet requests as they arise.

Nancy Reynolds Verney has expressed this point of view. "If we are to be useful to North Carolina, we must be able to respond to needs which are brought to our attention," she explained. "We could not do this if our income was 'frozen,' so to speak, in commitments to particular projects."

The Foundation began to broaden the base of its allocations in 1952. Until that year, it had concentrated on major undertakings: first the venereal disease control program, then the Smith Reynolds Airport at Winston-Salem, then the location of Wake Forest College at Winston-Salem. At the 1952 meeting of the trustees, several requests were presented by L. D. Long and William R. Lybrook as ones which W. N. Reynolds would have been likely to aid, had he been alive. These included $25,000 to help build a

Charles A. Cannon, Jr., Memorial Hospital, Banner Elk

hospital in Stokes County and $25,000 towards the construction of a library at Lees-McRae College, Banner Elk.

The trust established by the will of W. N. Reynolds increased the Foundation's income and made possible a growing number of such localized grants. This brought, naturally, a rising flow of requests to the Foundation.

While these grants have been widespread, they have never been random. All applications for aid have been sifted and studied, with critical attention to need and to probable results. The trustees have shown a marked tendency to help those who help themselves. Sometimes this is done by means of a challenge gift: an amount promised in the event a matching sum can be raised locally. However, the Foundation has not made a practice of setting difficult conditions for its help. It has looked with special favor on those situations where its contribution can mean the difference between success and failure for a venture, such as a local hospital or a needed college improvement.

One constructive role the Foundation has played in several instances has been to supply what Charles H. Babcock, one of the trustees, calls "seed money" to begin a worth-while enterprise which then can generate its own power. He cited as an example the North Carolina Foundation of Church-Related Colleges, which got its start in 1954 with the aid of the Z. Smith Reynolds Foundation. For three years, $15,000 per year was provided to the fledgling organization for overhead expenses. It has grown into a highly successful annual giving campaign among corporations to benefit church-related colleges of the state.

The Foundation has given a strengthening hand to construction projects, at both hospitals and colleges. This represents "brick-and-mortar" money, particularly vital in a burgeoning area such as North Carolina. Babcock pointed out that capital funds often are hard to come by for small colleges, or in underdeveloped communities. "In new areas, as the South is, it is important, I think, that there is 'brick-and-mortar' money here. In other parts of the country, colleges can get huge funds through capital campaigns among their wealthy alumni. Down here, many of the small colleges, especially the church-related ones, are training teachers, ministers, professional people, and capital just isn't available from their alumni for a new library facility, or a new science laboratory," he explained.

This is the gap the Z. Smith Reynolds Foundation has helped to fill for a long list of North Carolina institutions and communities.

Colleges that have received aid from the Foundation (aside from sustained programs such as those at Wake Forest, Davidson, the University of North Carolina at Greensboro, etc.) have included Appalachian State Teachers College, Boone; Atlantic Christian College, Wilson; Barber-Scotia College, Concord; Belmont Abbey College, Belmont; Bennett College, Greensboro; Brevard College, Brevard; Chowan College, Murfreesboro; Elon College, Elon College; Gardner-Webb College, Boiling Springs; Greensboro College, Greensboro; Guilford College, Greensboro; Livingstone College, Salisbury; Lees-McRae College, Banner Elk; Louisburg College, Louisburg; Methodist College, Fayetteville; North Carolina Wesleyan College, Rocky Mount; Pfeiffer College, Misenheimer; Queens College, Charlotte; St. Andrews College, Laurinburg; St. Augustine's College, Raleigh; Shaw University, Raleigh; Salem College, Winston-Salem; Southeastern Baptist Theological Seminary, Wake Forest; Warren Wilson College, Swannanoa; Western Carolina College, Cullowhee.

These include both tax-supported and private institutions, as well as church-related colleges of several denominations.

Schools that have benefited from the Foundation's generosity have included Asheville School, Christ School at Arden, Glade Valley School, Palmer Memorial Institute at Sedalia, Patterson

The library at St. Andrews College, Laurinburg

School, and Summit School. Grandfather Home for Children, an orphanage, has also been helped.

Better health for the people of North Carolina has been a Foundation concern from the beginning. It has expressed this concern repeatedly through grants to hospitals and health facilities in communities throughout the state. Sometimes this has been an allocation towards construction, and has run to several hundred thousand dollars. Again, it has been a grant for air conditioning or for X-ray equipment, and the amount has been small.

The Foundation's affinity with Winston-Salem has given a special priority to health needs in the area. Late in 1963, it committed itself to support in the amount of $1,500,000 for the Medical Center Development Program at the Bowman Gray School of Medicine and North Carolina Baptist Hospital. This expansion and development program will greatly strengthen the region's resources for medical care.

Other Foundation grants to health facilities in Winston-Salem include $500,000 to the Forsyth Memorial Hospital and $568,583.29 to North Carolina Baptist Hospitals, Inc.

A reference to the list of grants in the Appendix will show the large number of communities in which hospitals or other health care facilities have been aided by the Foundation. In addition, ways in which it has contributed to state-wide good health have included $75,000 to the North Carolina Hospital Education and Research Foundation, Inc., for a recruitment program for young people in health careers and $22,700 to recruit and train registered pharmacists for hospital service; $2,000 to the North Carolina Conference for Social Service for literature on prenatal care to be distributed throughout the state; $5,000 to the Medical Foundation of North Carolina, Chapel Hill, for its extension program for graduate nurses, and $600 to the same foundation toward the publication of a directory of North Carolina health organizations.

Aside from health, the Winston-Salem community has benefited in many ways from the Foundation's generosity and sense of civic responsibility. Grants have ranged from $200,000 for the Winston-Salem Coliseum and $200,000 for the modernization of Reynolds Auditorium to $6,000 for band uniforms for the Richard J. Reynolds High School and $10,000 towards the observance of the city's 200th anniversary, in 1966. Again, these are given individually in the list of allocations in the Appendix.

Of course, many of the grants to agencies located in Winston-Salem have a state-wide impact and should not be considered as local. An example is Old Salem, Inc., the restoration of the pioneer Moravian community which draws school children from all over the state, and visitors from the nation and world. The Foundation provided $100,000 for the project in 1960, and made available $151,615 in 1966 for the restoration of the Winkler Bakery. It also has aided the Moravian Music Foundation and made available $23,000 to the North Carolina Department of Archives and History for publication of three volumes of *Records of the Moravians in North Carolina.*

A similar case is the Goodwill Rehabilitation Center, Inc., which received $50,000 in 1962. Although located in Winston-Salem, its services are provided for handicapped persons from all North Carolina. It is now the largest Goodwill Center in the nation.

From time to time, the Z. Smith Reynolds Foundation has joined with other groups to give support and encouragement to special causes. It contributed $25,000 to the University of North Carolina towards launching an educational television program in 1953. Another occasion of supplemental aid to the University was $10,000 allocated in 1960 to underwrite the salary of a professor in the Institute of Field Physics.

The Foundation granted $20,000 to the Durham Child Guidance Clinic in 1960 towards construction of the clinic's new building. It provided $10,000 for the Cerebral Palsy and Rehabilitation Center of Raleigh in 1961 towards the cost of new facilities. The Greensboro Cerebral Palsy Association received $5,000 in 1963 to help in the expansion and renovation of its school and center.

Public library construction has been aided by the Foundation in the towns of Elkin, Liberty, Smithfield, Southport, Roanoke Rapids, and Yanceyville.

A program of leadership training for farm people is supported by a $25,000 grant to the North Carolina State Grange, which established the Leadership Training Fund in memory of the late W. N. Reynolds.

The trustees of the Foundation have shown an eagerness to extend their reach as much as possible over the whole of North Carolina. Applications have been encouraged from any community, any organization or institution, that feels it has a program for the improvement of the social well-being of the state's people. Naturally, this means that many proposals which are studied must be rejected, some of them worthy of support although they do not fit into the pattern of the Foundation's activity, or there simply is a lack of funds. Even so, it is only through this kind of examination of avenues of improvement that the Foundation can find the most effective uses for its resources.

The process of application has been kept simple. The Z. Smith Reynolds Foundation is a nonprofit, tax-exempt foundation whose grants are limited to the accomplishment of charitable works in North Carolina. Therefore, all applicants should be able to present evidence of a nonprofit, tax-exempt status.

No standard form of application is required, but all applications should be signed by an authorized person or official of the organization submitting the request. A letter is sufficient as an application, without copies, typed on standard letter-size paper. This should state the purpose for which assistance is requested, the total cost, the amount already on hand or pledged, and the amount requested. The letter should include any other information that the applicant feels would be helpful to the trustees in their consid-

Doctor and young patient at Babies' Hospital, Wrightsville Beach

THE Z. SMITH REYNOLDS FOUNDATION   83

eration of the request. All applications should be addressed to the Foundation's office, Wachovia Building, Winston-Salem.

Applications are processed and presented to the trustees, generally at meetings in the spring and fall. Requests are studied and discussed by the trustees, who then make their decisions.

THE FORWARD PATH   X

A FUTURE OF WIDENING SERVICE to North Carolina lies ahead for the Z. Smith Reynolds Foundation. Only a look to the past is necessary to confirm the forecast.

Its first three decades have seen phenomenal growth for the Foundation, in terms of resources, experience, and achievements. From the beginning in 1937 with the initial venereal disease control grant of $100,000, then regarded as munificent, the Foundation moved to total allocations of $2,864,600 in 1964. Nineteen separate projects shared the amount that year.

So, the Foundation will be able to do more in the years ahead simply because it has more with which to do. In the beginning, it received income from approximately $7,500,000. This figure has now reached $75,000,000. Based on a healthy U.S. economy and continued prudent management, the Foundation's level of income should be maintained, if not increased.

The Foundation will be able to do more because it knows more about how to do the work it sets for itself. Its leadership is seasoned. A pattern of operation has been evolved over the years, with some trial and error, suited to its role as promoter and supporter for health, education, and social improvements in North Carolina.

A partnership approach has enabled the Foundation to increase its capacity for service. In particular, it has worked in joint projects with the Mary Reynolds Babcock Foundation, established from the estate of one of the founders of the Z. Smith Reynolds Foundation. Close ties of family and mutual interest permit the trustees of both foundations an enlarged vision and a greater scope for accomplishment.

New directions have challenged the Z. Smith Reynolds Foundation as it has found itself in a position of increasing strength. As rising resources have freed it from consuming commitments, its trustees have looked about for effective ways to assure a fuller life for North Carolinians in the twentieth century.

No better instance could be cited than its participation in the North Carolina Fund, an ambitious effort to "break the cycle of poverty" by enriching opportunities for young people born into deprived circumstances.

The proposal was brought before the trustees early in 1963 by Terry Sanford, then governor of the state, who has recalled the inception of the North Carolina Fund in this way:

> The mosaic of ideas about how to combat the very incipience of poverty in our midst was fitted together from great minds from about the state and the nation; educational experiments in New Haven and Oakland, foundation projects in Boston and Washington, and a dozen other sites across America. But the great story in building an anti-poverty rationale for education was the community of interest we met from North Carolina citizens. One of the most dynamic and fruitful responses was struck in Winston-Salem and [with] the Z. Smith Reynolds Foundation and the Mary Reynolds Babcock Foundation— no strangers to remedial projects. From conversation with Mrs. H. Frank Forsyth, Charles Babcock, Mrs. Nancy Reynolds Verney, even a trans-Atlantic telephone call to R. J. Reynolds, Jr., and many other contacts, we received the enthusiasm and momentum that would inevitably be translated into action.

Mere political avowal of lofty goals has not been the tone of the sixties; so it was with our attitude toward the dark shadow of poverty.

There had to be fresh approaches, bold experiments, and, most of all, strong cooperation—from the tiniest rural hamlet to the centers of government and institutions.

The burden of responsibility, we reasoned, ought to be carried mainly by local leadership, with state and federal agencies interlocked to provide efficient cooperative services. The intermediary administrative device for coordinating this delivery, by education, of our children from poverty, would be "The North Carolina Fund," chartered in July of 1963. Private and non-profit, rather than a state agency, this control group was to have flexibility to gather in sympathetic moneys and to experiment with the greatest possible degree of freedom. It was "to concentrate on experimental action programs . . . to encourage comprehensive community projects . . . to encourage experimental projects by state agencies . . . to encourage local governments and community agencies to re-examine critically what they are doing and determine how new ideas and new approaches can produce better results." The Fund, in short, was the symbol of our belief that education is the best instrument for breaking the cycle of poverty. Its formula was regarded as viable by the prospective sponsors: The Ford Foundation made a grant of $7,000,000 in September of 1963; the Z. Smith Reynolds Foundation committed $1,625,000; and the Mary Reynolds Babcock Foundation, $875,000. This, in tandem with matching community support, gave us altogether some $14,000,000 for an action program spanning five years. Soon afterward pilot projects were spawned in a few selected communities across our State; there was a ferment of local initiative and public enterprise; and the North Carolina Fund was a going concern.

And in retrospect, I suppose one of my happiest thoughts is that, with the North Carolina Fund we have seen an individual state constructively exercising its responsibilities as a vanguard beacon for the federal government, not as its laggard antagonist. And just as proudly, I remember those early creative hours with the people of the Z. Smith Reynolds Foundation when the idea of the North Carolina Fund was barely a diamond in the rough.

When President Johnson prepared his "war on poverty" at the national level, he looked to North Carolina for a model. "Copies of the booklet outlining the North Carolina plan have become dog-eared in recent weeks as Federal planners have sought ideas on how best to combat poverty," reported a Washington dispatch in the *New York Times* on March 18, 1964.

"Even President Johnson has taken notice that North Carolina is ahead of the Federal Government," the article continued.

" 'I want to congratulate you on your initiative in mobilizing for an attack on poverty in North Carolina,' the President said in a message to state leaders in January.

"Months before poverty became the subject of a Federal campaign, plans for the North Carolina program were under way with funds supplied by the Ford Foundation, the Z. Smith Reynolds Foundation, and the Mary Reynolds Babcock Foundation."

Anne Reynolds Forsyth, one of the Foundation's trustees, was named to the board of directors of the North Carolina Fund. She was elected president of the board in 1966. After reviewing proposals for community action programs, the Board of Directors selected eleven programs for grants. These eleven involve twenty of the state's one hundred counties. The eleven community projects launched by the Fund are as follows: Urban-rural—Nash and Edgecombe counties; Craven County; Richmond, Robeson, and Scotland counties; Rowan County. Rural—Watauga, Avery, Mitchell, and Yancey counties; Macon County; Bertie, Halifax, Northampton, and Hertford counties. Urban—Forsyth County; Mecklenburg County; Durham County; and Buncombe County. The projects embrace a variety of experimental programs attacking the root causes of poverty in order to make people more self-reliant and better able to assume productive roles in the community.

The bold enterprise of the North Carolina Fund, bringing together private foundations and governmental agencies, has fired the public imagination and raised bright expectations. "I am quite excited about it," said Nancy Reynolds Verney. "I feel it represents a basic sort of approach to the problems we have been working with all the time. If we can help young people develop their own resources, it will have quite an uplifting effect."

It is experimental, she acknowledged, and many years may be required to show tangible results. Yet it represents the kind of search in which the Foundation must involve itself, she added, if it is to have a vital role in the state's affairs.

The expanding place of leisure in contemporary life has led the Foundation in some other new directions. It has recognized culture as a valuable part of social health and public education.

Two grants in 1964 aided cultural undertakings. One provided $300,000 towards a dormitory for the North Carolina School of the Arts. This institution, located in Winston-Salem, is projected as a training ground for talented youngsters in drama, the dance, and vocal and instrumental music—in fact, all the performing arts.

The other made available $15,000 to the University of North Carolina at Greensboro to cover any deficit in bringing the National Repertory Theatre to the campus for a period of rehearsal and performance. The visit served to stimulate students and faculty in the drama department, through contact with professionals. Actors and directors lectured to classes, and students watched the actual preparation of a drama. The wider public benefited, too, through the opportunity to see important plays well produced and performed.

Of course, Foundation grants in previous years had supported projects in cultural fields. The renovation of Reynolds Auditorium in Winston-Salem, as the community's concert center, would have to be regarded in this light. So would the allocation of $5,000 to the Moravian Music Foundation in 1957.

Still, the 1964 grants did represent a step towards the support of projects more specifically cultural. As such, they may have set a precedent for the future.

Growth increases responsibility. The Foundation's strengthened ability to serve North Carolina carries an obligation to see that resources are spent wisely and to the best advantage. As requests for aid mount, coming from all sections of the state, the job of the trustees becomes more and more demanding. Obviously, the task is one that calls for fully informed and expert opinion in deciding between pleas for help.

The trustees took action to meet the situation in 1964. They approved a resolution authorizing the president of the Foundation to appoint, with the approval of the trustees, two committees to advise on grants and allocations. One committee will deal with Education and Scholarships. The other will concern itself with Medical and Hospital Affairs. Each will have three or more members and a chairman designated by the president of the Foundation with the approval of the trustees. The Foundation's secretary will attend all committee sessions, prepare minutes, and supply them to the trustees.

Initial appointments to these committees were as follows: Medical and Hospital Committee: Joseph W. Lineberger, Belmont, chairman; Marshall I. Pickens, secretary of the Duke Endowment, Charlotte; and William F. Henderson, executive secretary of the N.C. Medical Care Commission, Raleigh. Educational Committee: Dr. Hollis Edens, executive secretary of the Mary Reynolds Babcock Foundation, Winston-Salem, chairman; Dr. William C. Archie, director for the N.C. State Board of Higher Education, Raleigh; and George H. Esser, Jr., executive director of the North Carolina Fund, Durham.

It is contemplated that committee members, persons of knowledge and authority in their fields, will be able to guide the Foundation in the allocation of funds for the greatest benefit of the people of North Carolina.

Its first thirty years have brought shining accomplishments for the Z. Smith Reynolds Foundation. Yet, in its new strength and in the demonstrated determination of its trustees to use that strength wisely, clearly the future holds promise of even brighter things to come.

APPENDIX I

Trustees of the Z. Smith Reynolds Foundation, 1936-1966

THE THREE INCORPORATORS of the Foundation, R. J. Reynolds, Jr., Mary Reynolds Babcock, and Nancy Reynolds Verney, were named lifetime trustees.

W. N. Reynolds, their uncle, was also an original trustee and continued to serve until his death on September 10, 1951.

The Foundation trustees include a representative of the Mercantile–Safe Deposit and Trust Company, Baltimore, Maryland, which is trustee for the Z. Smith Reynolds Trust. William R. Hubner, vice-president in charge of the trust department, served in this capacity until his death in 1948. He was followed by Thomas B. Butler, chairman of the board of directors of Mercantile–Safe Deposit and Trust Company.

Mrs. Verney was elected president of the Foundation at the meeting of the trustees on October 19, 1964. She makes her home in Greenwich, Connecticut, but frequently visits in Winston-Salem and North Carolina. She carries an active role in health, welfare, and other philanthropic works.

Charles H. Babcock is a vice-president of the Foundation, and has served as a trustee since 1946. Babcock is also president and treasurer of the Mary Reynolds Babcock Foundation, created from the estate of his first wife. He is a senior partner of Reynolds & Company, stockbrokers.

William R. Lybrook, also a vice-president of the Foundation, has been a trustee since 1953. He is vice-president and secretary of the R. J. Reynolds Tobacco Company. An attorney, he earned his degrees at Duke University and lives at Clemmons, near Winston-Salem.

Anne Reynolds Forsyth is the daughter of Z. Smith and Anne

Trustees of the Z. Smith Reynolds Foundation, 1967. Standing, left to right, L. D. Long, William R. Lybrook, and Charles H. Babcock; seated, left to right, Anne Reynolds Forsyth and Nancy Reynolds Verney; inset, left to right, Katharine Babcock Mountcastle, Joseph W. Lineberger, Smith Walker Bagley, Zachary Taylor Smith, and Thomas B. Butler.

Cannon Reynolds. She was elected in 1958 as a trustee of the Foundation established as a memorial to her father. She is married to Dr. H. Frank Forsyth, a prominent Winston-Salem orthopedic surgeon. Mrs. Forsyth is very active in local and state civic and social welfare programs.

Smith Walker Bagley has served as a Foundation trustee since 1959. He lives in Winston-Salem and is a vice-president of the Northwestern Bank. He is active in the Democratic Party and in public service. He is the son of Nancy Reynolds Verney and Henry Walker Bagley.

L. D. Long, a Foundation trustee since 1946, is a native of Alamance County, North Carolina. He has made his home in Winston-Salem for many years. Long was closely associated with W. N. Reynolds for many years.

Three trustees were elected on October 21, 1966. They are Katharine Babcock Mountcastle, Joseph W. Lineberger, and Zachary Taylor Smith.

Mrs. Mountcastle is the daughter of Charles H. Babcock and the late Mary Reynolds Babcock. She is a trustee of the Mary Reynolds Babcock Foundation and a director of the American branch of International Social Service. She is married to Kenneth Mountcastle, and they live in Darien, Connecticut.

Lineberger is a member of a family prominent in North Carolina's textile industry. He has served on the Gaston County Board of Commissioners and as a board member of the Gaston Memorial Hospital, in addition to many other activities in the area of public service.

Smith is assistant treasurer of the R. J. Reynolds Tobacco Company and active in Winston-Salem civic and cultural affairs. A native of Mount Airy, he is a graduate of the University of North Carolina at Chapel Hill.

Former trustees include R. Stratton Coyner, who served from 1954 to 1959, and Henry Walker Bagley, whose service ran from 1946 to 1953. Coyner, personal attorney to R. J. Reynolds, Jr., also filled the post of Foundation secretary from 1936 to 1959. Ledyard S. Staples has served as Foundation secretary from 1959 until the present.

Speech by Dr. Harold W. Tribble, President of Wake Forest College, on the Unveiling of the Zachary Smith Reynolds Portrait

(ON MAY 8, 1964, Wake Forest College unveiled a portrait of Zachary Smith Reynolds in the college library which is named in his honor. The trustees and administration of the college commissioned artist Joe King to paint the portrait, to hang permanently in the library as an expression of the college's gratitude to the Z. Smith Reynolds Foundation. The remarks by President Harold W. Tribble on the occasion of the unveiling are included here because they captured so well the spirit and philosophy of the Foundation in its service to the people of North Carolina.)

There is a symbolic significance in this occasion, with art, philanthropy, and education collaborating in harnessing one of the most inspiring attributes of human nature, the spirit of adventure.

Zachary Smith Reynolds was flying at the age of sixteen, about one year younger than the average freshman at Wake Forest College. His pilot's license was signed by Orville Wright, one of the pioneers in American aviation. He earned his transport pilot's license at seventeen, and he was at that time the youngest transport pilot in the United States. Two years later he flew from London to China in an 80-horsepower amphibian plane. When we compare aviation in 1931 with the achievements and proposals of the present space age, the imagination is thrilled by the symbolism of blending the adventuring spirit of a young aviator with the spirit of research and learning that boldly seeks to thrust back the frontiers of knowledge.

Matching his daring spirit that took him in fragile planes above the clouds was the unselfish spirit of his sisters and brother in dedicating their inheritance from his estate to the establishment of a philanthropic foundation in his name. In addition to many other worthy projects of positive leadership in promoting human welfare, the Trustees of the Z. Smith Reynolds Foundation conceived an adventure into the field of Christian higher education, challenging Wake Forest College to transplant century-old roots to the Winston-Salem community and bring old traditions into line with the educational demands of the modern world. In doing this the Foundation did not confront the College with a blueprint, or undertake to chart a course for the school, but contented itself with offering a vision and creating an opportunity.

Wake Forest College responded to the challenge. In fact, it demonstrated courageous vision on its own part in daring to move from a worthy past to a new and uncharted future. The College initiated a self-study, criticized its work, and projected its own renaissance. The result was a master plan for the campus that soon began to take shape in landscape and buildings, a blueprint of high ideals and exacting demands in dedication to the cause of excellence in education, and a demanding regimen of self-discipline and self-development.

So here we see three symbolic demonstrations of a noble spirit of adventure merging into a creative motivation: a young man in his teens who dared to put clouds beneath his feet; a family that dares to rise above self-interest, believing that wealth can be transmuted into wisdom; and a College that dares to transcend provincialism when truth commands.

It was this motivation that led to the offer and acceptance of financial support in 1946, to the beginning of construction of basic buildings in 1951, to the removal to this beautiful new campus in 1956, to the rebirth of the old school in its new home, and to the determination to rise steadily to genuine greatness in educational service.

Central to the life and purpose of our educational program is the Library, which was named the Z. Smith Reynolds Library in grateful recognition of what the Foundation has meant to the development of the College and in honor of him for whom the Foundation is named.

In further appreciation the Trustees and Administration of the College asked for the privilege of having a portrait of Zachary Smith Reynolds painted which would hang permanently in the Library.

For all of this Wake Forest College registers profound gratitude and pledges strong dedication to the realization of the greater vision of 1964 and beyond.

APPENDIX III

Procedure for Requesting Grants

THE Z. SMITH REYNOLDS FOUNDATION, INC., is a nonprofit, tax-exempt foundation whose grants are limited to the accomplishment of charitable works in North Carolina. All applicants for grants should be able to present evidence of a nonprofit, tax-exempt status.

No standard form of application is required, but all applications should be signed by an authorized person or official of the organization making the request.

A letter, without copies, typed on standard letter-size paper, stating the purpose for which assistance is needed, the total cost, the amount already on hand or pledged, and the amount of the request, is sufficient. The letter should include any other information it is felt would be of help to the Trustees in their consideration of the request.

All applications should be addressed to the foundation, Wachovia Building, Winston-Salem, or to one of the individual trustees.

APPENDIX IV

Z. Smith Reynolds Foundation, Inc. Grants and Appropriations Authorized 1936–1964

Year	To Whom Made	Amount	Total
1937	N.C. State Health Department, venereal disease control program	$ 100,000.00	
			$ 100,000.00
1939	N.C. State Health Department, venereal disease control program	160,000.00	
			160,000.00
1940	N.C. State Health Department, venereal disease control program	200,000.00	
	Forsyth County, airport development	150,000.00	
			350,000.00
1941	N.C. State Health Department, venereal disease control program	175,000.00	
	Forsyth County, airport development	80,000.00	
			255,000.00
1942	N.C. State Health Department, venereal disease control program	175,000.00	
	Health Publicity and Educational Program	4,500.00	
	Forsyth County, airport development	109,000.00	
			288,500.00
1943	Forsyth County, airport development	295,000.00	
	N.C. State Health Department, venereal disease control program	200,000.00	
	N.C. State Health Department, venereal disease control program (for 1944)	200,000.00	
			695,000.00

APPENDIX IV

Year	To Whom Made	Amount	Total
1945	N.C. State Health Department, venereal disease control program	$ 200,000.00	$
	Venereal Disease Education Institute	1,500.00	
			201,500.00
1946	N.C. State Health Department, venereal disease control program	125,000.00	
	N.C. Social Hygiene Society	75,000.00	
			200,000.00
1948	N.C. Social Hygiene Society	100,000.00	
	Wake Forest College, under 1946 contract	308,019.28	
			408,019.28
1949	Wake Forest College, under 1946 contract	330,538.57	
			330,538.57
1950	Wake Forest College, under 1946 contract	398,761.68	
			398,761.68
1951	Wake Forest College, under 1946 contract	613,106.52	
			613,106.52
1952	Stokes County, to aid hospital construction	25,000.00	
	Forsyth County, to aid construction of building housing agriculture and home demonstration agencies	25,000.00	

100   THE Z. SMITH REYNOLDS FOUNDATION

APPENDIX IV

Year	To Whom Made	Amount	Total
1952 Cont.	Lees-McRae College, to aid library construction	$ 25,000.00	$
	Winston-Salem Foundation, cattle barn for Forsyth County Fairgrounds	5,213.84	
	Winston-Salem State College, to continue W. N. Reynolds scholarship awards	500.00	
	Winston-Salem Coliseum Building Fund	100,000.00	
	Wake Forest College Building Fund	1,500,000.00	
	Wake Forest College, under 1946 contract	350,000.00	
			2,030,713.84
1953	University of North Carolina, educational television	25,000.00	
	Glade Valley School, girls' dormitories	25,000.00	
	Reynolds Park Fund, renovation and remodeling	35,000.00	
	Winston-Salem Coliseum Building Fund	100,000.00	
	Glade Valley School, boys' dormitories	40,000.00	
	North Carolina Baptist Hospital, construction aid	343,583.29	
	William and Kate B. Reynolds Memorial Park (Tanglewood), swimming pool and other park development	175,000.00	
	Wake Forest College, under 1946 contract	350,000.00	
			1,093,583.29
1954	North Carolina Foundation of Church Related Colleges, Inc., aid in launching Foundation	15,000.00	

APPENDIX IV

Year	To Whom Made	Amount	Total
1954 Cont.	Red Shield Boys Club, Winston-Salem, swimming pool	$ 20,000.00	$
	Wake Forest College, under 1946 contract	350,000.00	
			385,000.00
1955	Northern Surry County Hospital, Mt. Airy, construction aid	71,500.00	
	Winston-Salem State College, W. N. Reynolds scholarship awards	500.00	
	N.C. Foundation of Church Related Colleges, Inc.	15,000.00	
	City of Winston-Salem, completion of baseball park	30,000.00	
	William and Kate B. Reynolds Memorial Park, development	78,300.00	
	Wake Forest College, under 1946 contract	500,000.00	
			695,300.00
1956	Martin Memorial Hospital, Mt. Airy, X-ray and other equipment	35,000.00	
	N.C. Foundation of Church Related Colleges, Inc.	15,000.00	
	Nancy Jane Cox Reynolds Memorial School, vocational and agricultural building	35,000.00	
	City of Winston-Salem, baseball park building fund	15,000.00	
	N.C. Conference for Social Service, prenatal care literature	2,000.00	
	Consolidated Presbyterian College of North Carolina (St. Andrews), building fund	100,000.00	

102   THE Z. SMITH REYNOLDS FOUNDATION

APPENDIX IV

Year	To Whom Made	Amount	Total
1956 Cont.	Summit School, gymnasium building fund	$ 15,000.00	$
	Bowman Gray School of Medicine, building fund	250,000.00	
	Salem College, endowment for teachers' salaries	100,000.00	
	Lees-McRae College, building fund	50,000.00	
	William and Kate B. Reynolds Memorial Park, golf course	100,000.00	
	Wake Forest College, under 1946 contract	500,000.00	
			1,217,000.00
1957	William and Kate B. Reynolds Memorial Park, golf course	175,000.00	
	James E. Shepard Memorial Foundation, Inc., scholarships at North Carolina College at Durham	4,000.00	
	Winston-Salem Foundation, Dixie Classic Fair	50,000.00	
	Medical Foundation of North Carolina, Inc., extension program for graduate nurses	5,000.00	
	Moravian Music Foundation, program of research and publication	5,000.00	
	North Carolina Baptist Hospital, Winston-Salem, cobalt therapy	25,000.00	
	Southeastern Baptist Theological Seminary, Wake Forest, child care building	50,000.00	
	Medical Scholarships at Bowman Gray School of Medicine	151,200.00	

APPENDIX IV

Year	To Whom Made	Amount	Total
1957 Cont.	Grace Hartley Memorial Hospital, Inc., Banner Elk, construction aid	$ 100,000.00	$
	Wake Forest College, under 1946 contract	500,000.00	
			1,065,200.00
1958	Winston-Salem State College, faculty scholarships	15,000.00	
	Medical Scholarships at Bowman Gray School of Medicine	151,200.00	
	N.C. State Alumni Association, renovation of alumni building	100,000.00	
	Richard J. Reynolds High School, Winston-Salem, band uniforms	6,000.00	
	Albemarle Hospital, Inc., Elizabeth City, construction aid	176,000.00	
	Nancy Jane Cox Reynolds High School, Stokes County, scholarship program	6,000.00	
	William and Kate B. Reynolds Memorial Park, development	70,000.00	
	Wake Forest College, under 1946 contract	500,000.00	
			1,024,200.00
1959	Wake Forest College, girls' dormitory	750,000.00	
	Medical Scholarships at Bowman Gray School of Medicine	151,200.00	
	N.C. State University, faculty center	500,000.00	
	William and Kate B. Reynolds Memorial Park, development	200,000.00	

Year	To Whom Made	Amount	Total
1959 Cont.	Davidson College, professorships	$ 450,000.00	$
	Guilford College, auditorium construction aid	100,000.00	
	Livingstone College, Salisbury, women's dormitory	50,000.00	
	Chowan Hospital, Edenton, air conditioning	30,000.00	
	Lincoln Hospital, Durham, X-ray equipment	5,000.00	
	Yancey Hospital, Inc., Burnsville, X-ray equipment	11,000.00	
	Smith Reynolds Airport, restore mural painting	1,000.00	
	Valdese General Hospital, nursing home remodeling	138,383.00	
	Swain County Hospital, Inc., Bryson City, remodeling	8,000.00	
	Alamance General Hospital, Burlington, construction aid	50,000.00	
	Alexander County Hospital, Taylorsville, remodeling	6,000.00	
	Appalachian State Teachers College, Boone, book store addition	25,000.00	
	Grandfather Home for Children, Banner Elk, heating plant and repairs	50,000.00	
	Central Carolina Convalescent Hospital, Inc., Greensboro, remodeling	7,000.00	
	Nancy Jane Cox Reynolds High School, scholarships	6,000.00	

APPENDIX IV

Year	To Whom Made	Amount	Total
1959 Cont.	Medical Foundation of North Carolina, Inc., towards publication of a directory of N.C. health organizations	$ 600.00	$
	Wake Forest College, under 1946 contract	500,000.00	
			3,039,183.00
1960	Bowman Gray School of Medicine, Moore-Pruitt-Meredith Surgical Transfusion Research Fund	35,000.00	
	Bertie County Memorial Hospital, Windsor, X-ray equipment	12,000.00	
	Bladen County Hospital, Elizabethtown, X-ray equipment	12,000.00	
	Bowman Gray School of Medicine, purchase of books for library	75,000.00	
	Cape Fear Memorial Hospital, Inc., Wilmington, room furnishings	9,200.00	
	Davis Hospital, Statesville, expansion of School of Nursing	40,000.00	
	J. Arthur Dosher Memorial Hospital, Southport, X-ray equipment	12,000.00	
	Mountain Sanitarium and Hospital, Fletcher, construction aid	50,000.00	
	Pitt County Memorial Hospital, Inc., Greenville, equipment	12,000.00	
	Richmond County Memorial Hospital, Inc., Rockingham, X-ray equipment	12,000.00	
	Roanoke-Chowan Hospital, Ahoskie, towards expansion program	26,500.00	

APPENDIX IV

Year	To Whom Made	Amount	Total
1960 Cont.	Southeastern General Hospital, Inc., Lumberton, towards expansion program	$ 25,000.00	$
	Stokes-Reynolds Memorial Hospital, Danbury, X-ray equipment and emergency electric plant	25,000.00	
	Washington County Hospital, Plymouth, X-ray equipment	12,000.00	
	Gardner-Webb College, Boiling Springs, construction aid for science building	10,000.00	
	Queens College, Charlotte, supplemental endowment for professorship	100,000.00	
	Lees-McRae College, Banner Elk, construction aid for science building	50,000.00	
	Livingstone College, Salisbury, girls' dormitory	50,000.00	
	Pfeiffer College, Misenheimer, modern language laboratory	15,000.00	
	Salem College, Winston-Salem, unrestricted endowment	100,000.00	
	Western Carolina College, Cullowhee, pilot program with gifted children	35,000.00	
	Durham Child Guidance Clinic, Durham, construction aid	20,000.00	
	North Carolina State Grange, W. N. Reynolds Leadership Training Fund	25,000.00	
	Old Salem, Inc., Winston-Salem, endowment	100,000.00	
	Medical Scholarships at Bowman Gray School of Medicine	151,200.00	

APPENDIX IV

Year	To Whom Made	Amount	Total
1960 Cont.	Nancy Jane Cox Reynolds High School, scholarships	$ 6,000.00	$
	Appropriation for a general survey of colleges in North Carolina	11,976.03	
	University of North Carolina, underwriting salary of a professor in the Institute of Field Physics	10,000.00	
	Winston-Salem Foundation, towards cost of new Forsyth General Hospital	500,000.00	
	Wake Forest College, under 1946 contract	500,000.00	
			2,041,876.03
1961	City of Winston-Salem, swimming pool and golf course, Winston Lake Park	125,000.00	
	N.C. State University, faculty center	300,000.00	
	Winston-Salem State College, W. N. Reynolds scholarship awards	500.00	
	Medical Scholarships at Bowman Gray School of Medicine	151,200.00	
	Nancy Jane Cox Reynolds High School, scholarships	6,000.00	
	William and Kate B. Reynolds Memorial Park, towards development	112,000.00	
	Wake Forest College, Life Sciences Building equipment	50,000.00	
	Summit School, expansion program	180,000.00	
	Bennett College, Greensboro, expansion program	100,000.00	

Year	To Whom Made	Amount	Total
1961 Cont.	Queens College, Charlotte, endowment for faculty salaries	$ 50,000.00	$
	St. Andrews College, Laurinburg, towards library and furnishings	42,000.00	
	Bowman Gray School of Medicine, Moore-Pruitt-Meredith Surgical Transfusion Research Fund	20,000.00	
	Western Carolina College, Cullowhee, pilot program for gifted children	17,168.00	
	Valley Clinic and Hospital, Bat Cave, physical therapy equipment	1,000.00	
	Alleghany County Memorial Hospital, Sparta, X-ray equipment	15,000.00	
	Garrett Memorial Hospital, Crossnore, operating room equipment	20,000.00	
	Moore Memorial Hospital, Inc., Pinehurst, expansion and addition	50,000.00	
	Winston-Salem Foundation, annual budget assistance	30,000.00	
	Roanoke Rapids Public Library, construction aid	15,000.00	
	N.C. Department of Archives & History, to assist restoration of building at Wake Forest, N.C., known as the birthplace of Wake Forest College	7,000.00	
	N.C. Department of Archives & History, for publication of two additional volumes of *Records of the Moravians in North Carolina*	15,000.00	
	Patterson School, Lenoir, building program aid	10,000.00	

APPENDIX IV

YEAR	TO WHOM MADE	AMOUNT	TOTAL
1961 Cont.	James E. Shepard Memorial Foundation, Inc., scholarships at North Carolina College, Durham	$ 4,000.00	$
	Cerebral Palsy and Rehabilitation Center, Raleigh, towards cost of rehabilitation facilities	10,000.00	
	Wake Forest College, under 1946 contract	500,000.00	
			1,830,868.00
1962	Wake Forest College, graduate school study	30,000.00	
	Medical Scholarships at Bowman Gray School of Medicine	151,200.00	
	N.C. State University, phytotron plant research facility	750,000.00	
	North Carolina Baptist Hospital, Inc., Winston-Salem, towards purchase of Kembly Inn property	200,000.00	
	Reynolds Auditorium, Winston-Salem, renovation	200,000.00	
	Smithfield Public Library, towards cost of new library	5,000.00	
	Appropriation for graduate school study	827.92	
	Katharine Smith Reynolds Scholarships, University of North Carolina at Greensboro	57,600.00	
	Expenses in connection with Katharine Smith Reynolds scholarships	987.05	
	Nancy Jane Cox Reynolds High School, scholarships	6,000.00	

APPENDIX IV

Year	To Whom Made	Amount	Total
1962 Cont.	Cape Fear Memorial Hospital, Inc., Wilmington, towards cost of addition and equipment	$ 25,000.00	$
	Hamlet Hospital and Training School for Nurses, Inc., Hamlet, towards cost of improvements	25,000.00	
	Lenoir Memorial Hospital, Inc., Kinston, towards improvement program	20,000.00	
	Lexington Memorial Hospital, Inc., Lexington, improvement program and X-ray equipment	25,000.00	
	Lincoln Hospital, Durham, medical education program	45,000.00	
	Memorial Mission Hospital, Asheville, expansion program	50,000.00	
	Pungo District Hospital Corporation, Belhaven, towards hospital addition	38,000.00	
	Scotland Memorial Hospital, Laurinburg, towards building program	50,000.00	
	Valley Clinic and Hospital, Bat Cave, renovations	2,600.00	
	Louisburg College, Louisburg, towards expansion program	15,000.00	
	St. Andrews College, Laurinburg, library building program	58,000.00	
	Salem College, Winston-Salem, building program	100,000.00	
	Winston-Salem State College, faculty scholarships	25,000.00	
	Camp Robert C. Vaughn, Winston-Salem, towards completing the camp	50,000.00	

APPENDIX IV

YEAR	TO WHOM MADE	AMOUNT	TOTAL
1962 Cont.	Goodwill Rehabilitation Center, Inc., Winston-Salem, towards new building	$ 50,000.00	$
	N.C. Hospital Education and Research Foundation, recruitment program among young people for careers in health	75,000.00	
	Wake Forest College, under 1946 contract	500,000.00	
			2,555,214.97
1963	Medical Scholarships at Bowman Gray School of Medicine	151,200.00	
	Roanoke-Chowan Hospital, Ahoskie, X-ray equipment	11,000.00	
	Rutherford Hospital, Inc., Rutherfordton, X-ray equipment and vehicle for student nurses	27,000.00	
	William and Kate B. Reynolds Memorial Park, development program	100,000.00	
	North Carolina Fund	650,000.00	
	Katharine Smith Reynolds Scholarships	57,600.00	
	Expenses relative to Katharine Smith Reynolds Scholarships	999.95	
	Nancy Jane Cox Reynolds High School, scholarships	6,000.00	
	Chowan Hospital, Edenton, towards chronic and convalescent nursing home	10,000.00	
	Davie County Hospital, Mocksville, hospital addition	25,000.00	
	Greensboro Cerebral Palsy Association, towards expansion and renovation	5,000.00	

APPENDIX IV

Year	To Whom Made	Amount	Total
1963 Cont.	Maria Parham Hospital, Henderson, towards cost of new hospital	$ 50,000.00	$
	Martin General Hospital, Williamston, X-ray equipment	5,000.00	
	Bowman Gray–Baptist Hospital Medical Center	600,000.00	
	Our Community Hospital, Scotland Neck, heating plant and other repairs	5,000.00	
	Asheville School, Asheville, five-year development program	5,000.00	
	Christ School, Arden, for library	30,000.00	
	Salem College, Winston-Salem, towards auditorium–fine arts center	75,000.00	
	Johnston County Public Library, Smithfield, towards new building	10,000.00	
	Wake Forest College, under 1946 contract	500,000.00	
			2,323,799.95
1964	Medical Scholarships at Bowman Gray School of Medicine	150,000.00	
	Davidson College, endowment	500,000.00	
	College Foundation, Inc., Raleigh, capital funds for student loan plan	50,000.00	
	University of North Carolina at Greensboro, to support National Repertory Theatre visit	15,000.00	
	200th Anniversary General Committee, Winston-Salem	10,000.00	
	N.C. School for Performing Arts, dormitory	300,000.00	

APPENDIX IV

Year	To Whom Made	Amount	Total
1964 Cont.	Katharine Smith Reynolds Scholarships	$ 57,600.00	$
	Expenses relative to Katharine Smith Reynolds Scholarships	1,000.00	
	Nancy Jane Cox Reynolds Memorial Scholarships	12,000.00	
	The North Carolina Fund	325,000.00	
	Bowman Gray–Baptist Hospital Medical Center	400,000.00	
	Bennett College and Livingstone College Scholarships	100,000.00	
	Annie Penn Memorial Hospital, Reidsville, expansion program	25,000.00	
	Babies' Hospital, Inc., Wilmington, expansion program	15,000.00	
	Caldwell Memorial Hospital, Lenoir, expansion program	50,000.00	
	Blowing Rock Hospital, towards additions and renovations	100,000.00	
	Methodist College, Fayetteville, towards new administration building	50,000.00	
	Palmer Memorial Institute, Sedalia, boys' dormitory	150,000.00	
	St. Augustine's College, Raleigh, library addition	54,000.00	
	Wake Forest College, under 1946 contract	500,000.00	
			2,864,600.00
1965	University of North Carolina at Greensboro, to support National Repertory Theatre visit	10,000.00	

APPENDIX IV

YEAR	TO WHOM MADE	AMOUNT	TOTAL
1965 Cont.	Katharine Smith Reynolds Scholarships	$ 57,600.00	$
	Expenses relative to Katharine Smith Reynolds Scholarships	4,400.00	
	Nancy Jane Cox Reynolds Memorial Scholarships	12,000.00	
	Davidson College Endowment	750,000.00	
	Bowman Gray School of Medicine and North Carolina Baptist Hospital, for Medical Center Development Program	500,000.00	
	Carteret General Hospital, Morehead City, elevator and emergency generator for new hospital	35,000.00	
	Charles A. Cannon, Jr., Memorial Hospital, Inc., Banner Elk, X-ray equipment	24,000.00	
	Forsyth Memorial Hospital, Winston-Salem, establishment and operation for three years of School of Medical Technology	47,400.00	
	Lincoln County, towards operational expenses of proposed new hospital	25,000.00	
	Memorial Mission Hospital, Asheville, expansion and renovation project	25,000.00	
	N.C. Hospital Education and Research Foundation, Inc., Raleigh, to recruit and train registered pharmacists for hospital service	22,700.00	
	Pungo District Hospital Corporation, Belhaven, dietary addition	10,000.00	
	Barber-Scotia College, Concord, purchase of books	15,000.00	

APPENDIX IV

YEAR	TO WHOM MADE	AMOUNT	TOTAL
1965 Cont.	Belmont Abbey College, Belmont, for new science building	$ 50,000.00	$
	Z. Smith Reynolds Foundation Scholarships	100,000.00	
	Medical Scholarships at Bowman Gray School of Medicine	150,000.00	
	Garrett Memorial Hospital, Crossnore, X-ray equipment	15,000.00	
	Hatteras Medical Center, Hatteras, to assist in establishment of new Medical Center	20,000.00	
	Pender Memorial Hospital, Inc., Burgaw, towards cost of new hospital	33,000.00	
	Watauga County Hospital, Boone, towards cost of new hospital	50,000.00	
	Wilmith Hospital, Charlotte, towards cost of new hospital	10,000.00	
	Atlantic Christian College, Wilson, for enlarging library facilities	25,000.00	
	Chowan College, Murfreesboro, for construction of new library	25,000.00	
	Elon College, Elon College, N.C., for construction of new library	25,000.00	
	Salem College, Winston-Salem, for South Hall restoration	35,000.00	
	Warren Wilson College, Swannanoa, for expansion of library collection and science departments	25,000.00	

APPENDIX IV

Year	To Whom Made	Amount	Total
1965 Cont.	N.C. Department of Archives & History, for publication of Volume XI *Records of the Moravians in North Carolina*	$ 8,000.00	$
	Hyconeechee Regional Library, Yanceyville, equipment for the Caswell County Public Library	11,500.00	
	Town of Liberty, to assist new library project	10,000.00	
	Bishop McGuinness Memorial High School, Winston-Salem, development of athletic field	5,000.00	
	Greensboro College, Greensboro, for new humanities building	75,000.00	
	Livingstone College, Salisbury, for Ten-Year Development Program	25,000.00	
	N.C. Wesleyan College, Rocky Mount, for new library building	25,000.00	
	Greensboro College, Greensboro, Historical Book Club of N.C., Inc., program	10,000.00	
	N.C. 4-H Development Fund, Inc., various projects	25,000.00	
	State of North Carolina, for swimming pool at State Home and Industrial School for Girls, Eagle Springs	12,000.00	
	Wake Forest College Birthplace Society, Inc., Wake Forest, restoration of building	5,000.00	
			2,312,600.00

APPENDIX IV

Year	To Whom Made	Amount	Total
1966	Reynolda House, Inc., Winston-Salem, permanent collection of paintings and sculpture	$ 100,000.00	$
	Medical Scholarships at Bowman Gray School of Medicine	150,000.00	
	Blowing Rock Hospital, Blowing Rock, expansion program	45,000.00	
	North Carolina Eye-Bank, Inc., Winston-Salem, headquarters building of Eye-Bank Association of America and N.C. Eye-Bank	5,000.00	
	Swain County Hospital, Inc., Bryson City, expansion program	50,000.00	
	Pfeiffer College, Misenheimer, for new library building	50,000.00	
	Shaw University, Raleigh, for purchasing and improving adjacent property	100,000.00	
	Brevard College, Brevard, development program	50,000.00	
	Bertie County Development Association, Windsor, books for new library	5,000.00	
	Brevard Music Center, Brevard, expansion and renovation program	10,000.00	
	Elkin Library Building Fund, Elkin, for new library	30,000.00	
	Grandfather Home for Children, Banner Elk, new water system	10,000.00	
	Institute of Government, The University of North Carolina, Chapel Hill, for research project on new forms and records		

APPENDIX IV

Year	To Whom Made	Amount	Total
1966 Cont.	for use in offices of the Clerks of Superior Court under the Judicial Department Act of 1965	$ 22,518.00	$
	Public Library of Southport and Brunswick County, Southport, towards cost of new library	10,000.00	
	Winston-Salem State College, W. N. Reynolds Scholarship awards	100.00	
	Katharine Smith Reynolds Scholarships	57,600.00	
	Expenses relative to Katharine Smith Reynolds Scholarships	1,000.00	
	Nancy Jane Cox Reynolds Memorial Scholarships	12,000.00	
	The North Carolina Fund	650,000.00	
	Davidson College, Davidson, endowment	625,000.00	
	Old Salem, Inc., Winston-Salem, restoration of Winkler Bakery	151,615.00	
	North Carolina School of the Arts, expansion program	200,000.00	
	North Carolina Board of Higher Education, Raleigh, computer orientation project	25,000.00	
	The Summit School, Winston-Salem, purchase of adjoining property	30,000.00	
	District Memorial Hospital of Southwestern North Carolina, Andrews, towards cost of addition	50,000.00	
			2,439,833.00
			$30,919,398.13